Christmas 1979

The Pride of Portland

The Pride of Portland

The Story of the Trail Blazers

by
Frank Coffey
and
Tom Biracree

EVEREST HOUSE

Publishers   New York

Library of Congress Cataloging in Publication Data

Coffey, Frank.
The pride of Portland.

1. Portland Trail Blazers (Basketball Team)—
History.   I. Biracree, Tom, 1947–   joint author.
II. Title.
GV885.52.P67C63   1979   796.32'364'0979549   78-57408
ISBN 0-89696-007-2

Copyright © 1979 by Frank Coffey and Tom Biracree
All Rights Reserved
Library of Congress Catalog Card Number: 78-57408
ISBN: 0-89696-007-2
Published simultaneously in Canada by
Beaverbooks, Pickering, Ontario
Manufactured in the United States of America by
American Book–Stratford Press, Inc.
Saddle Brook, New Jersey
Designed by Sam Gantt
First Edition

CONTENTS

Introduction   *vii*

SECTION ONE: THAT CHAMPIONSHIP SEASON

1. The Building of a Champion   *3*
2. The 1976–77 Regular Season   *13*
3. The 1977 NBA Playoffs   *29*
4. Round One: Portland Trail Blazers vs. Chicago Bulls   *33*
5. Round Two: Portland Trail Blazers vs. Denver Nuggets   *43*
6. Round Three: Portland Trail Blazers vs. Los Angeles Lakers   *55*
7. Round Four: Portland Trail Blazers vs. Philadelphia 76ers   *69*

SECTION TWO: PROFILES OF THE CHAMPIONS

8. Jack Ramsay   *103*
9. Bill Walton   *110*
10. Maurice Lucas   *134*
11. Bob Gross   *146*
12. The Guards   *151*
13. The Reserves   *161*

Contents

SECTION THREE: THE FALL FROM THE THRONE

14. The 1977–78 Season — *173*
15. The 1978 Playoffs — *183*
16. The 1978–79 Season: Controversy and Challenge — *191*
17. The 1979 Playoffs — *199*

Appendix I: The Trail Blazers Year by Year — *202*
Appendix II: Portland Trail Blazer Statistics — *215*

INTRODUCTION

*I*N 1978, in the midst of one of the most successful seasons ever enjoyed by a professional basketball team, the defending National Basketball Association champion Portland Trail Blazers had suddenly been struck by an almost unprecedented blizzard of injuries that effectively blighted their chances for a second successive crown. On May 1, 1978, the favored Seattle Supersonics defeated the Trail Blazers 105–94, knocking Portland out of the playoffs with a four games to two quarter final round victory.

But this series was one of those rare events in sports history in which the defeat of a defending champion was not the most important story. Bob Ryan of the Boston *Globe,* one of the most astute commentators on basketball, summed it up: "If the spirit of competition has any meaning left in professional sports, then the Portland Trail Blazers performed more like champions this year than they did last. In an era of selfish, whining professional athletes, the Blazers reminded us all of the way it is supposed to be." Syndicated basketball colunmnist Peter Vecsey put it another way: "Physiologists tell us it is impossible to play your heart out. That shows you how ill acquainted they are with the Portland Trail Blazers." Other basketball writers around the nation wrote similar pieces, using the same words over and over again: self-sacrifice; courage; teamwork; dedication; hard work.

Of course, like "honesty" in politics and "modesty" in the movie business, such terms are often nothing more than lip service, self-applied by professional sports teams basking in the warm glow of success. But in sports, and especially in professional basketball, fortunes change with the twist of a knee, the blow of a whistle, or the hiring of a new agent. All too often, in adversity, teamwork and self-sacrifice give way to the kind of self-interest and bickering that dominate today's sports pages.

The tidal wave of injuries that devastated Portland in 1978 continued into 1979. And with it came the bitter accusations of star center Bill Walton. Such a controversy as the Walton case alone would have torn other franchises asunder. But, amazingly, in spite of this succession of blows, the Trail Blazer basketball team stuck to its system, each active member continuing to play selflessly and to the maximum of his ability. In 1978 the Blazers won two games against a healthy Seattle team that advanced to the NBA finals that year and won the NBA crown in 1979. This past season, the Blazers again reached the playoffs, where they succumbed to the powerful Phoenix Suns only in the last quarter of the last game.

Off the court, Portland dealt with adversity like a championship franchise. Despite all the accusations of wrongdoing, no witch-hunt was conducted, no scapegoat was fired to shunt criticism. And the fans that filled the Memorial Coliseum in better times still filled that arena to the rafters, demonstrating anew that the phenomenon called Blazermania was a kind of team support that was more positive and joyful than the kind of mindless partisanship

Introduction

so often seen in other cities. Although the Maurice Poduloff Championship trophy had moved on to Washington in 1978 and Seattle in 1979, Portland remained in many ways the home of basketball champions.

When the Trail Blazers, who had plodded through six barely mediocre NBA seasons, rose to capture their 1977 crown, their sudden good fortune seemed to be a miracle. But the incredible cohesiveness shown during the last two seasons soundly belies that easy explanation. Today, even more so than in the spring of 1977, one clearly sees that Portland's championship, like most significant human achievements, came about when men of unusual vision, through the application of intelligence and the assistance of Lady Luck, were able to assemble a group of talented people willing to work together toward a common end—the building of a team capable of not only winning one NBA championship but of dominating professional basketball for years to come.

The fact that such an audacious goal was not immediately realized testifies to the difficulty of the task. In the past ten years, no team has successfully defended its NBA championship, as compared to three defenders in baseball, two in football, and two in hockey. In a game of intricate teamwork, the loss of just one of the eleven men on the roster can be damaging, and the loss of two or more can be fatal. The inevitable injuries caused by the rigors of an 82-game schedule, combined with the temptations offered by free agentry, make success as an NBA franchise the most fragile of accomplishments. In light of the above, the record of the Trail Blazers over the last three seasons has convinced many observers that the City of Roses is fortunate to have one of the most remarkable and stable franchises in all of professional sport.

The Pride of Portland, a history of the Blazers, centers around the fascinating story of how this marvelous basket-

Introduction

ball team was assembled and how it waged the struggle for the 1977 NBA crown. Among the characters are colorful, talented men whose names and achievements will still be in the memories of basketball fans for decades to come. But even more important than men is the character of a franchise, and the adherence to an overriding common vision. This book begins with that vision.

ONE

THAT CHAMPIONSHIP SEASON

1
THE BUILDING OF A CHAMPION

*E*VEN BEFORE THE ADVENT of the Trail Blazers, the word "pride" came easily to the lips when speaking of Portland, Oregon. The City of Roses sits astride the Willamette River, at the western portal of the scenic Columbia River Gorge. In the distance, snow-capped Mount Hood rises majestically from a lovely, green, rolling carpet of Douglas firs. Few American cities can boast such natural beauty at their doorstep.

Portland was founded in 1845 by 821 fortunate souls who named the city after Portland, Maine, rather than Boston, Massachusetts, the decision made by the flip of a coin. The population reached 50,000 by the turn of the century, then increased sevenfold by 1950.

Unlike that of other urban areas, however, this growth was accomplished gracefully. Good government, good planning, and just plain community goodwill allowed Portland to maintain a quality of life that the Midwest Research Council called the "highest" of any urban area in the country.

In such an idyllic setting, great dreams came easily. In

The Pride of Portland

particular, Oregonians' love of the outdoors meant a love of sports, and many talked of bringing major professional sports to Portland.

The man who held most firmly to this vision was a University of Oregon graduate named Harry Glickman. After promoting boxing during the postwar period, Glickman set out on a campaign to bring a professional basketball team to Oregon. In the beginning, however, he had little success. Faced with rising costs of travel and talent, the NBA was moving out of the smaller cities that had been its first homes—out of Rochester and Fort Wayne in 1957, out of Syracuse in 1963. Despite Glickman's efforts and arguments, the NBA owners felt Portland couldn't support major professional sports.

Glickman, however, didn't give up. He recognized that no franchise could succeed without generating sufficient dollars at the box office to be competitive. He set out to prove that Portland would respond. His professional football exhibitions drew record crowds. He obtained a franchise in the Western Hockey League, and his Portland Buckaroos won seven regular season and three playoff titles in nine years.

Finally, in early 1970, ABA-NBA merger talks fell through, and the NBA voted to expand. The persistent Harry Glickman was awarded a precious franchise for the City of Roses.

Glickman sooned proved to be as able a basketball executive as there was in the league. Portland attendance climbed for five seasons from 145,000 to 441,000. Unlike many expansion franchises, the Trail Blazers rested on rock-solid financial ground.

But making money was not Glickman's primary concern. In a team meeting in the fall of 1971, the Blazers' executive vice-president held up his hand and told his players, "This is a championship ring from the Portland

Buckaroos. My dream—and it should be yours—is to wear one for the Portland Trail Blazers."

Many of the members of the Portland organization in those days didn't share that dream, and they soon departed. One believer was Stuart Inman, who had signed on as a temporary scout to put the very first Portland team on the floor in 1970. In the middle of the 1971–72 season Inman took over as interim coach from Rolland Todd, then was named vice-president of player personnel, joining Glickman in what was to become the first stage in the dream—a championship front office.

The first test of the ability of a front office staff is results in the NBA draft. Attention becomes riveted on this annual auction, fans speculating endlessly on the proper first round choice.

In many ways, however, it is not the first round but the rest of the draft that separates a good from an exceptional judge of talent. In this respect, Harry Glickman and Stu Inman have compiled a record that places their names up with Red Auerbach's in modern basketball.

Of all the statistics connected with Portland's rise to glory in professional basketball, not one bodes better for the future of the franchise than the following: On the 12-man roster of the 1977–78 Portland Trail Blazers were no fewer than six players drafted by Portland *after* the first round. The kind of judging expertise that fact represents is absolutely astounding.

Of course, amid the later round choices were some significant first round selections—Geoff Petrie, Sidney Wicks, and most of all, Bill Walton. The signing of Walton, after a tension-filled coin toss with Philadelphia and a sealed bidding duel with San Diego of the ABA, seemed, to most fans, to mean that long-sought-for success on the court was in reach. But injuries to Walton and team personality conflicts smothered enthusiasm. For the first time in the franchise's history, attendance fell in 1975–76, and fans began to boo the team. With his usual perspicacity, Glickman knew there was a problem, but he refused to give in to midseason pressure to hastily trade Sidney Wicks or fire Lenny Wilkens. He said, "A lot of times when you get into a situation like ours, you trade apples for oranges just to do something. And that is something we don't intend to do."

What Glickman and Inman did intend to do first was go out and hire a coach who best fulfilled their three main requirements: a fierce determination to win; a strong record of achievement; and, most importantly, a commitment to team basketball. They found the perfect man in Jack Ramsay.

Ramsay, an articulate, candid, intelligent man who holds a doctorate in education from the University of Pennsylvania, had demonstrated great ability in his very first major assignment. In 1955, taking over the reigns of a St. Joseph's College team that had gone 12–14 the year before, he produced a 23–6 mark. In his 11 years at the Philadelphia school, he compiled a sparkling 234–72 record and led his team into ten NCAA tournaments. He then became general manager of the NBA champion Philadelphia 76ers, and subsequently coached the team for four seasons. In 1972 he moved to Buffalo, an expansion team that entered the NBA the same year as Portland. After one losing season, he led the Braves to three successive winning seasons and three successive playoff appearances.

Ramsay's dedication to superb physical conditioning and his reservations about Bob McAdoo and Ernie Digregorio caused problems with Buffalo owner Paul Snyder. When Ramsay became available, Portland quickly signed him aboard.

After ten years of intense study of NBA basketball, Ramsay had developed a system based on two central concepts: aggressive, pressure defense and fast break offense.

The Pride of Portland

Ramsay believed that defense set the pace of a game, and was the major determinant in the success of an NBA team. Pressure, beginning at midcourt, intensified the tempo of a game, made the other team work harder to get into its offensive set, and generated turnovers.

All offense in the NBA is based on obtaining physical advantage, or mismatches. The easiest way to obtain a mismatch is to beat the opposing team down the floor on a fast break, getting a two on one or three on two opportunity. If the mismatch isn't available, Ramsay believed, the break began movement that converted into the kind of sharp cutting and passing patterned offense that generated the maximum number of high percentage shots.

Pressure defense and fast break offense required a starting lineup of five players who fit five specific roles:

1. The dominant center: In the two decades prior to 1977, only one team has won a championship without one of the following dominant centers—Bill Russell, Wilt Chamberlain, Kareem Abdul-Jabbar, Willis Reed, Dave Cowens. The center first of all is a ferocious defender, clogging the middle, blocking shots. His rebounding and outlet passes key the fast break. If the fast break is denied, the center keys a patterned offense, passing off skillfully or shooting from the low post.

2. The power forward: Another intimidator who prevents the opposition from ganging up on the center, and a strong rebounder who also throws skillful outlet passes. In patterned play, the power forward sets smartly positioned, sturdy picks from which his teammates can "brush off" their defenders to create uncontested jump shots or height mismatches.

3. The small or shooting forward: This player's prime requirements are the quickness to fill a lane on the

fast break, great movement without the ball, and a strong outside shot to prevent the defense from collapsing on the big men. In today's NBA, this player must have the strength to guard an Adrian Dantley, the quickness to check a Julius Erving.

4. The point or small guard: This player is the second coach on the court, the leader of the fast break. He must have the ball handling ability to beat any press, and he must be an excellent penetrator who enjoys passing off to an open teammate once inside ten feet.

5. The big or shooting guard: He must have the quickness to run the break and a fine outside shot that prevents sagging defenses. Furthermore, the big guard often finds himself checking the opposing team's high scorer, and his defensive ability is crucial.

After the starting five, Ramsay felt a championship team needed backup players who could fit into one of the specific roles above. A team with two small playmaking guards on the bench gets into trouble when its starting shooting guard gets into foul trouble checking a Doug Collins or George Gervin. A team with no adequate substitute at power forward can be worn down by a big, physical club like the Washington Bullets. With the grueling physical demands of the 82-game NBA schedule, balance on the bench is as important as balance in the starting lineup.

Finally, a team that has the talent will still not be a winner if the players don't understand and accept their roles. Said Jack Ramsay, "Every team in the NBA has great players. But raw ability is going to win only a few games. It's combined ability that wins."

When Jack Ramsay got to Portland, he found that Stu Inman had provided him with a number of players to fill

The Pride of Portland

key roles on his kind of team. Most important of all was the dominant center. From the moment of his appointment as coach, Ramsay announced, "I'm a Walton man." He flew to Portland, sat down with the big redhead, and discovered he and Walton had many things in common. Walton shared Ramsay's commitment to team basketball—he'd proven that in high school, then at UCLA. The bickering and ball hogging of the Portland teams in his first two years disgusted him. Second, he shared Ramsay's intensity and his fierce determination to win. Third, he appreciated Ramsay's personality—candid, low key, based on the firm belief that sports have to be placed in perspective. Furthermore, Ramsay was a health nut, a firm believer in physical conditioning and natural foods. Walton joined Ramsay on long bike rides through the hills around Portland, and approached the 1976–77 season with renewed enthusiasm. Ramsay had his center.

When Ramsay joined the Blazers, he could hardly recall an unheralded player from Long Beach State named Bob Gross. Ramsay looked at the films, then decided Gross was his small forward. No one worked harder at running offensive plays, no one hustled more on defense, no one had better shot selection. Most important, no one had his speed and quickness to fill the lane on a fast break.

A third sure starter in the Ramsay system was big guard Lionel Hollins. Hollins was a fine shooter who in college had run the blistering fast break of Arizona State. Inman had drafted him for his quickness and intelligence. After some problems early in his rookie year, Hollins was rapidly becoming a superior defensive guard.

A coin flip in 1974 and two shrewd draft choices had given Portland three of its five key role players. Now a similar mixture of luck and keen judgment was to provide the other two. Part of the luck came with the ABA-NBA merger, and the folding of the Virginia franchise. Inman

The Pride of Portland

had drafted a 6'1" guard from Old Dominion named Dave Twardzik in 1972. Twardzik had rejected the Blazers' offer at that time, preferring to stay near home. Now he was available again, and Inman, as high on him as ever, rushed to sign the experienced, speedy playmaker and penetrator. Ramsay had his small guard.

An element of luck also entered into the filling of the vital power forward slot. The merger resulted in a dispersal draft of players from the folding teams who did not belong to an NBA club. Chicago had the first choice, and it was known they were going to select big center Artis Gilmore. Atlanta had the second selection, and the obvious choice was the ABA's most feared enforcer, 6'9" Marquette alumnus Maurice Lucas. But Hubie Brown, just appointed Atlanta coach, had a violent personality conflict with Lucas when both were at Kentucky. Aware of this conflict, the Trail Blazers offered Geoff Petrie and Steve Hawes for Atlanta's selection. The Hawks took the bait in what was one of the shrewdest NBA trades of the decade. To pay for Lucas, Portland sold Sidney Wicks to the Boston Celtics.

Lucas provided far more than just strength and rebounding. He was an extremely intelligent player who had been thoroughly indoctrinated in team basketball by the brilliant Al McGuire at Marquette. His strong outside shooting was a large plus. Finally, he was a vegetarian who had become acquainted with Walton at the 1974 NCAA tournament. When Luke came to Portland, this acquaintance blossomed into a firm friendship that fired up both men.

His starting team assembled, Ramsay turned his attention to the vital reserves. Moses Malone, a multitalented but immature center-forward, had also been acquired in the ABA dispersal draft. As good as Malone's potential was, Ramsay felt he couldn't fill the kind of exact role he

The Pride of Portland

had in mind, and that the young man would quickly become unhappy sitting on the bench. Portland astutely dealt Malone to Buffalo for cash and a valuable 1978 first-round draft pick, with which they chose Mychal Thompson.

Portland did have some ideal reserves already on the roster. Larry Steele, the most veteran of the Blazers, was a consummate team player who had the size to play small forward, and the quickness to fill in against bigger guards. Lloyd Neal, runner-up to Bob McAdoo for rookie of the year in 1972-73, had the ability to start at power forward for some other teams; could fill in at center; and, again, was an unselfish player who always gave 100 percent.

The draft provided additional help. The key choice turned out to be third pick Johnny Davis, a lightning-quick guard from Dayton. In addition to being an ideal third guard on the fast break, Davis was an extraordinary leaper and penetrator. First choice Wally Walker was a fine shooter with good quickness who needed schooling in defense.

Six-year veteran Herm Gilliam, a good outside shooter with playoff experience, was purchased from Seattle on September 1. From Europe, the Blazers picked up backup center Robin Jones, who had the defensive ability to keep Portland in the game while Walton rested. The final niche was filled the night before the season opened, when the Lakers released four-year veteran Corky Calhoun, a defensive specialist who more than made up for the inexperience of the rookie Walker.

The Portland roster now contained 12 men selected not by name or reputation, but for their ability to fit and accept designed roles. Eight of the 1976-77 Trail Blazers were original Portland draft choices: Two came from trades or purchases; two were picked up as free agents. Not coincidently, 11 of the 12 had played for winning college teams selected for the NCAA tournament (Bob Gross's Long Beach State team was on probation and not eligible for postseason play).

In five months Portland had completed a remarkable restructuring. But the changes were not a mere face-lift, or an exchange of "apples for oranges." Rather, they were the culmination of years of careful planning designed to produce a team that would truly be the pride of Portland.

2

THE 1976–77 REGULAR SEASON

THE RESTRUCTURING of the Trail Blazers produced unprecedented interest and enthusiasm in Oregon as the 1976–77 NBA season approached. Season tickets sales soared 23 percent to 8,103. That total was the highest in the Pacific Division, and exceeded the average Portland attendance in the first four years of the franchise.

On Friday night, October 22, 1976, a record crowd of 12,626 jammed Memorial Coliseum. They leaped to their feet and roared as the Blazers took the floor for their opening game against the New York Nets.

Seven new faces wore the stylish red, black, and white jerseys. Gone were Geoff Petrie and Sidney Wicks, the former rookies of the year and stars of the early years. Gone too were Larue Martin, a former number one draft pick, Danny Anderson, Barry Clemens, Steve Hawes, and Steve Jones.

With so many unfamiliar faces, fans turned often to the Blazer program to match numbers to names. The 1976–77 Portland roster read this way:

The Pride of Portland

No.	Player	Pos.	Ht.	Wt.	Birth Date	Yrs.	College
10	Corky Calhoun	F	6'7"	212	10/ 1/50	4	Penn '72
16	Johnny Davis	G	6'2"	170	10/21/55	R	Dayton '76
3	Herm Gilliam	G	6'3"	192	4/ 5/47	7	Purdue '69
30	Bob Gross	F	6'6"	200	8/ 3/53	1	Lg. Beach '75
14	Lionel Hollins	G	6'3"	185	10/19/53	1	Ariz. St. '75
34	Robin Jones	C	6'9"	225	2/ 2/54	R	St. Louis '75
20	Maurice Lucas	F	6'9"	218	2/18/52	2	Marquette '74
36	Lloyd Neal	F	6'7"	225	12/10/50	4	Tenn. St. '72
15	Larry Steele	F–G	6'5"	191	5/ 5/49	5	Kentucky '71
13	Dave Twardzik	G	6'1"	180	9/20/50	4	Old Dom. '72
42	Wally Walker	F	6'7"	200	7/18/54	R	Virginia '76
32	Bill Walton	C	6'11"	225	11/ 5/52	2	UCLA '74

Head Coach: Jack Ramsay, St Joseph's '49
Asst. Coach: Jack McKinney, St. Joseph's '57
Trainer: Ron Culp, Bowling Green '68

There was no doubt in anyone's mind that the talent the Portland management had assembled would lift them out of the Pacific Division cellar. But basketball pundits pondered several critical questions in assessing how high the Blazers would vault.

Many of the questions centered around how well and how quickly the Blazers would adjust to Jack Ramsay's new system and to each other. Portland, last in the division in offense the year before, needed a dynamic fast break to overcome the loss of scoring from Wicks and Petrie. Could Lucas and Walton get the rebounds to trigger the break? Could the youthful guards avoid the turnovers and fouls that cripple an offense? How well could the team stick to their patterns when the break wasn't available?

Stamina was another problem. The kind of all-out, pressing, baseline-to-baseline game Ramsay wanted to play required rest for the starters. Could the reserves provide the level of performance and consistency in their ten to 20 minutes of playing time?

Perhaps, most of all, attention was focused on Bill Walton. The year before, the Blazers had won seven in a row when he was in peak form. Without him, they were the worst team in the league. Could the man who had sat out 78 games in two years stay healthy for an entire, grueling 82-game schedule? How would the rest of the team respond to even his brief absences from the lineup? And, finally, would some new controversy arise that would dampen his new intensity and enthusiasm?

The questions above made basketball analysts wary in making their predictions. Both *Sporting News* and *Sports Illustrated* concluded that Portland could rise no further than third. Said *Sporting News*'s Joe Gilmartin: "For the Blazers to show up in the NBA finals this year would be astonishing."

The competition the Trail Blazers faced made even rabid Portland fans cautious. For the second year in a row, the Pacific Division figured to be by far the strongest in the NBA. Golden State, NBA champions in 1974-75, had won the division by 16 games the year before. The Warriors led the league in scoring and in margin of victory in 1975-76. Returning were future Hall of Fame forward Rick Barry and smooth Jamaal Wilkes, backed up by the double-D musclemen, Dwight Davis and Derrick Dickey. At center, Clifford Ray and shot blocker George Johnson were joined by huge rookie Robert Parish from Centenary. The backcourt of Phil Smith, Charles Johnson, Charles Dudley, and Gus Williams was the quickest in the NBA.

The Phoenix Suns recovered from an early 4-18 stretch to reach the finals of the NBA championship in 1976. The Suns' rise was not miraculous. Rather, it was based on the rapid maturing of center Alvin Adams, whose team play and passing were reminiscent of Bill Walton. Dead-eye shooter Paul Westphal had been acquired from the Celtics for Charlie Scott in one of the best trades of the decade. Ricky Sobers, Garfield Heard, Keith Erickson, and the Van

The Pride of Portland

Arsdale brothers made up an able supporting crew that was greatly strengthened by the drafting of Oregon's Ron Lee. Lee, an incredible all-around athlete who had also been drafted by football's San Diego Chargers and soccer's Portland Timbers, earned the nickname Taz (for Tasmanian devil) due to his nonstop play and aggressiveness.

Bill Russell had led the Seattle Supersonics to the playoffs the year before. Center Tom Burleson and strong man Leonard Grey were a fearsome rebounding duo. Bald, colorful Slick Watts had led the NBA in steals and assists the year before. Many of his passes went to "Downtown" Freddy Brown, a gifted pure shooter who had averaged 23 points per game. Seattle backcourt defense had been bolstered by rookies Dennis Johnson and 6'7" Bob Wilkerson. With some additional front court support, observers felt, the Sonics would be playoff contenders again.

Finally, the Lakers were blessed with the awesome Kareem Abdul-Jabbar. Jabbar led the league in rebounds, blocked shots, minutes played, and was second in scoring the previous season, and despite a weak supporting cast, the Lakers had won 40 games. Kermet Washington, Don Ford, Earl Tatum, Cazzie Russell, Don Chaney, Lucius Allen, and Mack Calvin didn't sound like the roster of a 1977 title team, but no one could underestimate the basketball acumen and inspirational leadership of new coach Jerry West, perhaps the best guard who ever played the game.

The other divisions were strengthened by a wealth of players made available by the merger with the ABA. For the first time in years, there was no competition to sign draft choices, no threats to jump leagues. Veterans and rookies struggled fiercely for precious roster spots. Indiana, San Antonio, and, especially, the Denver Nuggets, brought experienced, powerful teams into the league. Only the

The Pride of Portland

New York Nets, Portland's opening night opponents, looked like doormats.

As the minutes ticked away toward 8:00 P.M. on that October 22, Portland fans knew that, for the first time, they had a team with the talent and a coach with the vision to be champions. Tonight, they could tell from the way the players slashed and dunked their way through warm-up drills that a new attitude had infused their Blazers. Jack Ramsay had said, "I have never seen a team at a professional level so willing to accept team principles. Our practices have really been good and it's like coaching a group of college kids." As the buzzer sounded and the teams approached center court, the only question was how well that team would fulfill its potential.

Their first game was not conclusive. The Nets, stripped of their front line by the loss of Julius Erving and the trading of Larry Kenon and Billy Paultz, hung within a point at halftime. In the third quarter, however, Lucas and Walton began ripping rebounds off the boards, and the fast break got rolling. Walton and Lucas finished with 32 boards, Johnny Davis came off the bench to toss in 19, and Portland breezed to a 114-104 win.

A far sterner test—the Golden State Warriors—arrived in town four days later. After a tight, defensive first quarter in which Portland built a seven-point lead, both teams ran for a combined total of 68 points in period two. After intermission, Golden State cut the Blazers' nine-point halftime lead to five. In years past this pressure would have triggered a Portland collapse. But Ramsay was able, this time, to go to his bench and call on the recently acquired veterans Herm Gilliam and Corky Calhoun. Calhoun and Gilliam combined for 18 third-quarter points that pushed the lead from five to 15 points, and the Blazers coasted to a 110-96 win. Walton had 19 rebounds, 21 points, and six blocked shots; Lionel Hollins had eight assists; and Bob Gross tossed in 14 points to go along with an outstanding defensive job on Rick Barry. It was beginning to look like the Trail Blazers were for real.

Enthusiasm was momentarily quelled as Rick Barry exploded for 34 points and Charles Dudley had 12 assists to lead the Warriors to a 112–92 homecourt victory over Portland on October 28. But then the Blazers returned home to smash Detroit 131–97. Next, they shot 62 percent in rolling to a 129–116 win over Atlanta. After the Trail Blazers had raced for a team record 45 first-quarter points, an irate Hawk coach Hubie Brown pointed at the scoreboard and screamed in frustration at his shell-shocked team, "Look up there. You know what that means? That means 180 damn points a game!"

The Trail Blazers had opened the 1975–76 season 0–4. This year they were 4–1, with the average margin of victory 18 points. Six players were shooting over .500. The dominant figure was Bill Walton, who averaged 17.3 rebounds, 19.5 points, 3.4 blocked shots, four assists, and most important, 37.2 minutes per game—22 minutes a game more than his average the preceding year.

Jack Ramsay talked about Walton: "I knew Bill was a great player, of course, but he has a great attitude which, to be honest, I wasn't aware of. You always want to keep an open mind about every player when you take over a new club, but naturally you hear things about a Walton.

"Bill was my first target when I came to Portland. I sought him out and came away convinced he wanted to play basketball, he wanted to play in Portland, he wanted to play on a winning team, he was willing to do whatever it takes to win."

In those first five games Walton had done what it takes to win. Then, on Friday night, November 5—Walton's twenty-fourth birthday—he did even more.

The Pride of Portland

The opponents that night were the Philadelphia 76ers. The fortunes of Philadelphia, NBA champs in 1966–67 and contenders under Jack Ramsay, had plummeted in the early 1970s. In the 1972–73 season, the Sixers managed only nine wins, the worst record in league history. Then, in came flamboyant owner F. Eugene Dixon, determined to dish out several of his multimillions to assemble a team with awesome individual talent. Three million went to George McGinnis, the muscular ABA all-star who averaged 23 points per game (ppg) in 1975–76. Six more million went to the incredible Julius Erving—three-time ABA Most Valuable Player; a 28.9 ppg career average; a man who, while perhaps the best one-on-one player in the history of the game, was still considered a team player. Dixon enticed Caldwell Jones from the ABA with a fat multiyear contract, then persuaded gigantic Darryl Dawkins to move directly from high school to the NBA. With defensive specialist Harvey Catchings, Philadelphia had the deepest center crew in the NBA.

At guard was Doug Collins, a 20.8 ppg scorer who moved without the ball better than any guard in the league. From New Orleans came steady, playmaking guard Henry Bibby. To come in off the bench were hot-shooting Lloyd ("All World") Free, Joe Bryant, and Steve Mix. In 1975–76, without Erving, Jones, or Bibby, the Sixers had taken four of four from the Trail Blazers.

But in this first meeting of 1976–77, the Trail Blazers never let the Sixers into the game. After another record crowd (12,823) serenaded Walton with a chorus of "Happy Birthday," the Blazers threw him a party. When the dust settled at the end of the first quarter, Portland led 41–27. They added 36 more in the second for a 26-point halftime lead, then 36 in the third for a 39-point lead after three. The final: 146–104. The total tied Portland's all-time best. Seven Blazers hit double figures. Walton was magnificent, leading the scoring with 26 points, snagging 16 rebounds, dishing out six assists. Dr. J did dazzle the crowd with some aerial acrobatics, and McGinnis and Collins got their 20. But no other Sixer reached double figures, and Portland's win was a triumph for team basketball.

Oregon's budding romance with the Blazers suddenly turned into a passionate love affair. Sellout or near sellout crowds watched the Blazers sprint to seven more consecutive home wins in November. The streak was capped by a 145–115 rout of Indiana, in which eight Blazers hit double figures and the team racked up a club record 59 field goals. The former cellar dwellers were perched on top of the Pacific Division, leading the league in scoring. Their pressure defense made them sixth in defense as well. Jack Ramsay was pleased: "I knew going in that we had the kind of players we wanted, but naturally felt it would take time to fit so many new players into a whole new system. I still feel that way, but I have to say we are way ahead of schedule."

The hesitancy implied in Ramsay's last sentence stemmed from one glaring problem—the team's failure to win on the road. At home, Portland played textbook basketball—in Ramsay's words, "If I wanted to give a clinic on how to run the fast break, I could show our home-game films." Away from the friendly confines of Memorial Coliseum, however, the Blazers were tentative and inconsistent. After a dismal first half at lowly Atlanta, they came back from a 16-point deficit only to fall to John Drew's 24-foot jump shot with three seconds left. George Gervin poured in 32 points on 11 for 15 shooting as the San Antonio Spurs dumped the Blazers two nights later. At New Orleans a second-quarter run-in with Dave Twardzik spurred Pistol Pete Maravich to a 35-point performance in a tough 100–98 Portland loss. On Friday, November 26, at Los Angeles against the Lakers, who were beginning to play marvelous basketball under Jerry West, Walton and

The Pride of Portland

Hollins led the Blazers to a hard-fought three-point third-quarter lead. But Kareem and Lucius Allen scored 18 points in the last quarter as the second-place Lakers clawed to a 99–96 win. Two days after scoring 145 points at home against Indiana, the Blazers dropped an embarrassing 116–105 game to Milwaukee, as only four players reached double figures.

Of course, bad games on the road were inevitable for a young team like the Blazers. And with the increased travel in a schedule that now included the four former ABA teams, home team winning percentage in the league had jumped from 64 percent to 73 percent, a record level. But even though the rest of the NBA was having problems away from home, Portland's 0–6 road record was a sign of potential trouble. A championship team must retain its poise in tight situations, and must pick up its share of road victories. Losses to tough championship contenders like San Antonio and Los Angeles were excusable. Embarrassing defeats by cellar dwellers like Atlanta and Milwaukee were, in Jack Ramsay's mind, definitely not.

On December 1, Dave Twardzik swished two free throws with six seconds left to give Portland a 101–100 win at Indiana. But the Blazers had let a 15-point halftime lead slip away, bleeding much of the satisfaction from the first road win. The rest of the NBA was still watching for the convincing road win that meant the Trail Blazers had truly arrived.

That win came on Friday, December 3, against the Phoenix Suns. Maybe it was a mass mirage, but the Blazers played as if the Arizona desert sands were the clean, green hills of home. Portland jumped to an early lead and twice built a 20-point margin. Maurice Lucas crashed the boards for 15 rebounds and added 20 points. Gross added 16, along with eight assists. Herm Gilliam came off the bench to score 21.

The Pride of Portland

But, once again, Bill Walton was at the heart of the victory. Phoenix pulled within seven early in the fourth quarter. Then, with the suddenness of tropical rain, Walton turned superman. With turnaround jumpers, hooks, and dunks, he scored 11 points in seven minutes to seal the 113–99 win.

After that victory, Curry Kirkpatrick of *Sports Illustrated* wrote that "Bill Walton has emerged as the best all-around basketball player in the world." Said Center Alvin Adams, "The guy just keeps storming at you. They should win the division easy." Walton led the NBA in rebounds and blocked shots. The Portland Trail Blazers, after six years of frustration and defeat, were at the top of the National Basketball Association with a 14–6 record.

The Blazers continued to play marvelous basketball during the last month of 1976. Wins over Milwaukee and Cleveland stretched the home win streak to 20 games. A four-game road trip began with Hollins and Johnny Davis running circles around Walt Frazier and Earl Monroe as the Blazers recorded their first-ever win in Madison Square Garden, 111–94. Sidney Wicks got some revenge against his former mates as his 13 third-quarter points led the Celtics to a 104–93 victory. But Jack Ramsay celebrated his return to Buffalo with a 103–102 win, and Bill Walton led a valiant effort at Philadelphia with 30 points before Julius Erving hit a 12-foot jumper with two seconds left to give the Sixers a 108–107 win.

Returning home, the Blazers chalked up season win number nineteen. Bob Gross tossed in 16 of his game-high 22 points in the first quarter as Houston fell 104–84. No previous Portland team had won 19 games before mid-January. A satisfying 127–105 win over Denver ran the home win streak to 22 games. But all good things must come to an end, and the coup de grâce was administered by the ferocious play of Kareem Abdul-Jabbar. Five days before, the cover of *Sports Illustrated* featured a photo of Walton with the caption "King Of The Mountain At Last." Evidently jacked up sky high by the article, Jabbar came out for the center jump without his goggles. In an incredible seesaw battle, the starting front line of the Blazers responded to Jabbar by scoring 72 points. Walton alone pulled down 26 rebounds. But Kareem matched their heroics, scoring six of his 35 points in overtime as the Blazers finally succumbed 115–111.

Undaunted, Portland started a new home streak with wins over Kansas City and Seattle, before finishing 1976 with a 1–3 road trip. Despite the losses, however, the Trail Blazers still looked down at the rest of the Pacific Division as they downed their well-deserved champagne on New Year's Eve:

Team	Won	Lost	Percentage	Games Behind
Portland	23	12	.657	—
Los Angeles	21	13	.618	1½
Golden State	16	15	.516	5
Seattle	18	19	.486	6
Phoenix	14	16	.467	6½

By this New Year's Eve, many of the questions asked by basketball analysts and Portland fans alike had been answered. The Blazers had adapted superbly to Jack Ramsay's system. Their fast break was textbook basketball, smooth, powerful, awesome. Their pressure defense intimidated opponents and created further opportunities for the break. The bench had responded so well to every challenge that Portland, for the first time in its history, was able to play a true 48-minute baseline-to-baseline game. The only problem had been consistency on the road, an inevitable consequence of going with such a young team.

As the Blazers prepared to entertain the Chicago Bulls on New Year's Day, however, a second problem arose. Bill

Walton would be forced to sit out his first game of the year, having twisted his knee in the December 30 road loss to Milwaukee.

Portland fans, watching Walton's marvelous play game after game, had almost forgotten his injury problems of the previous two seasons. Indeed, like all fans, they take for granted that their heroes can play day after day, just like they manage to make it to work. But the fact is that Walton's having played in 35 consecutive games was a marvelous achievement. No big man in the NBA plays at anywhere near 100 percent during the course of the season. The brutal pounding in the pivot makes muscle strains, pulls, bruises, and aches constant companions. For an athlete with Walton's intensity and previous medical problems—tendonitis in both knees since the age of 15, a history of foot problems, pin in his left wrist—playing so hard for 35 games demonstrated that he was a superbly conditioned athlete with acute sensitivity to the needs of his body.

While Walton rested, the rest of the team responded to the challenge by holding off the Bulls 89–82 in a tough defensive battle. Lloyd Neal led the Blazers with 20, and Lucas pulled down 13 rebounds. The next night, in Los Angeles, again without Walton, the Blazers roared to a 34–12 first-quarter lead behind the shooting of Maurice Lucas. Then Kareem took over, and the Lakers finally pulled it out 104–99. With the victory, LA went into a tie for first place with Portland.

Walton, his knees still aching, returned to the lineup as the Blazers headed back to Portland for a four-game home stand that was to represent the high point of the 1976–77 season. In seven days the Trail Blazers smashed Boston 128–84, New Orleans 130–118, San Antonio 150–113, and New York 131–111. During this stretch they averaged an astounding 134 points per game, and the total of 150

The Pride of Portland

against San Antonio was the high for the season. On January 11 their record was 28-13, their winning percentage .683, their lead over the surging Lakers, two games. The Blazers were 23-1 at home, averaging 118.2 points and yielding only 101.4—the difference of 17.3 was the best in the league.

On the road, however, the Blazers were a paltry 5-12, averaging only 100.9 and giving up 104.2. This amazing difference concerned Ramsay as the team started an eight-game road trip, the longest of the year. Walton's knees were still giving him problems. More seriously, Lionel Hollins, point man of the Blazer fast break, had sustained a fractured skull and would miss at least the first four games.

The road trip opened with a convincing 107-92 victory at Boston that spoiled Dave Cowens' return to the Celtics after his two-month sabbatical taken for "personal" reasons. On successive nights, the exhausted Blazers lost to Washington and Atlanta.

Three days rest and a date against the lowly New York Nets provided a much needed tonic. Furthermore, Lionel Hollins returned to the lineup with a fiber glass face mask like that worn by hockey goalies. Said Hollins, "It was frustrating. You can't see too well. It's hot, and nobody can hear you when you talk." At one point in the Blazers' 109-94 victory, Hollins, arguing with referee Joe Gushue, ripped off the mask like a baseball catcher outraged by an umpire's call.

The momentum of the Nets game carried through a win at Cleveland, before losses to Houston and San Antonio. Then the Blazers closed out the road trip by coming from a 19-point deficit to defeat Denver 107-102. Maurice Lucas had 22 points, 14 rebounds, and six assists to lead the Blazers to a victory that gave them a credible 4-4 road trip and kept them on top of the Pacific Division.

But returning home was a mixed blessing. During the

The Pride of Portland

trip, Bill Walton had developed an inflamed Achilles' tendon on his right foot. He managed to play in a 112–104 win over San Antonio, but then was forced to sit out ten games, and his importance to the success of the team became readily apparent. The Blazers managed a 97–91 home win over Phoenix. A 119–107 loss at Kansas City on February 2 dropped them out of first place in the Pacific Division for the first time all year. A road win at Indiana the next night, led by Lucas' 35 points, put them back in front. But three consecutive home losses to Washington, Denver, and Atlanta put LA back in front to stay. The game against the Hawks, the last-place team in the Central Division, was particularly painful, as they outscored the Blazers in every quarter en route to a convincing 121–108 win. As the Blazers took some badly needed rest at the All-Star Break, the Pacific Division standings were as follows:

Team	Won	Lost	Percentage	Games Behind
Los Angeles	35	19	.648	—
Portland	35	21	.625	1
Golden State	30	24	.556	5
Seattle	29	26	.527	6½
Phoenix	25	27	.481	9

The rest didn't do much good as the Blazers managed to salvage only one win over Chicago in a four-game road trip. But Walton returned to the starting lineup and victory in a hard-fought 113–111 home win over the Celtics that pulled Portland to within one game of LA. The best part of the victory was the 43-point performance of Lionel Hollins, who had been in a shooting slump since his skull fracture.

Walton's playing time remained limited as the Blazers lost to Central Division leader Houston 123–106. Heroic performances by Lucas (34 pts.), Hollins (26 pts.), and Larry Steele (16 pts.) led Portland to a 108–107 win over

The Pride of Portland

the Sixers, reversing the one-point loss at the Spectrum on December 11.

But the triumph was short-lived, as Walton again had to leave the lineup, this time with a left ankle sprain, and the Blazers dropped four out of five. For the first time all year, Blazer fans began to worry. The playoff spot that seemed clinched by mid-December now began to look shaky. Without Walton, Portland was 5–12, a .293 pace that would be, if extended to a full season, the second worst in the NBA. If Walton couldn't return to his previous form, the dream of so many Oregon fans would be shattered.

On March 15, at home against New Orleans, Walton returned and put all the doubts to rest. The Blazers smashed the Jazz 131–104, with Lucas and Hollins complementing Walton with 20 and 22 points respectively. Walton's in-

FINAL STANDINGS 1976–77

EASTERN CONFERENCE

Atlantic Division					Central Division				
* Philadelphia	50	32	.610	—	* Houston	49	33	.598	—
* Boston	44	38	.537	6	* Washington	48	34	.585	1
New York	40	42	.488	10	* San Antonio	44	38	.537	5
Buffalo	30	52	.366	20	* Cleveland	43	39	.524	6
Nets	22	60	.268	28	New Orleans	35	47	.427	14
					Atlanta	31	51	.378	18

WESTERN CONFERENCE

Midwest Division					Pacific Division				
* Denver	50	32	.610	—	* Los Angeles	53	29	.646	—
* Detroit	44	38	.537	6	* Portland	49	33	.598	4
* Chicago	44	38	.537	6	* Golden State	46	36	.561	7
Kansas City	40	42	.488	10	Seattle	40	42	.488	13
Indiana	36	46	.439	14	Phoenix	34	48	.415	19
Milwaukee	30	52	.366	20					

* Playoff teams

tense play after so long a struggle with physical problems demonstrated once again that he was an athlete with rare physical skills and rare personal courage.

The Blazers, with Walton in the lineup every game, only lost four more games the rest of the season. They prepared for their first-ever appearance in the playoffs with a final six-game win streak reminiscent of that tremendous four-game stretch in January. The final home game, played before an SRO crowd of 12,792, was a 145–116 rout of the league-leading Lakers, who had taken the previous three meetings between the teams. The NBA was served notice: The Portland Trail Blazers had no intention of making their first visit to the playoffs a short one. Only Walton's injuries, they felt, denied them a Pacific Division championship. With Walton healthy, their goal was nothing less than a National Basketball Association Championship Trophy.

3

THE 1977 NBA PLAYOFFS

ON APRIL 11, the eve of the opening game of the 1977 National Basketball Association Playoffs, Blazermania was at its peak. Playoff stories crowded other news off the state's newspapers and off the airways. Phones at Blazer offices rang off the hook as, it seemed, at least half of Oregon's 2 million citizens were trying to squeeze their way into Memorial Coliseum for what some enthusiastic observers were calling the most significant Oregon date since the Beaver State entered the Union on February 14, 1859. Fans were confident that Blazers would become the Pacific Northwest's first major sports champions since the Seattle Metropolitans downed the Montreal Canadiens in the finals of the 1917 National Hockey League playoffs.

The regular season had certainly provided many reasons for optimism. Reason number one was the play of Bill Walton. In Walton's 65 games the Blazers had been 44-21, a .677 percentage that, extended to a full season, would have been the best in the NBA. Walton led the NBA in rebounding (14.4) and blocked shots (3.35), the second Portland player ever to lead the league in a major category (the other was Larry Steele's steals crown in 1973–74). The big center shot 53 percent from the floor, 70 percent from the free throw line, and dished out 245 assists (to lead the NBA centers). His infectious enthusiasm and ceaseless struggle for perfection made him the ideal team captain.

Maurice Lucas had debuted in the NBA with an awesome year that led many observers to call him the premier power forward in the league. Luke was ninth in the league in rebounding with 11.4 per game average, and he and Walton made up by far the most potent rebounding combo in the game. Lucas led the Blazers in scoring with a 20.2 average, five more than his ABA average. He scored over 30 points in nine games. Most important, his fierce competitive attitude complemented Walton's, and his presence on the court prevented the kind of physical intimidation that can smother a fast break offense.

With the rebounding in such capable hands, Bob Gross was free to fill the lane on the fast break and concentrate on executing offensive plays. Gross was sixth in the NBA in shooting percentage (.529—an all-time Portland record). His free throw shooting jumped from 68 percent to 85 percent, and his assists skyrocketed to 242. His defense also improved, and with 81 starts, he demonstrated his durability.

The year 1976–77 was the one in which Lionel Hollins emerged as a star. Hollins led the Blazers with 313 assists and was sixth in the NBA in steals. His scoring average jumped from 10.8 to 14.7 points per game. He hit a season-high 43 points against the Celtics on February 2, and with the playoff berth on the line in March, he shot a blistering 56 percent in a five-game stretch.

Only one player in the NBA ever officially shot .600 or better in a single season. Wilt Chamberlain did it three times—.683 in 1966–67; .649 in 1971–72; and the NBA record .727 in 1972–73. In the past season, Dave Twardzik,

The Pride of Portland

who's a foot shorter than Wilt, shot .612, but he fell a scant 37 field goals short of qualification for NBA ranking. His astounding year included percentages of .813 against Denver and .750 against Seattle. Overall, he averaged 10.3 points per game, shot .842 from the free throw line, and handed out 247 assists.

The reserves outplayed everyone's expectations, led by Larry Steele. The most veteran Blazer averaged double figures for the first time in his career (10.3), shot 50 percent from the floor and 80 percent from the line, and scored over 20 points in six games. Herm Gilliam (9.3) and Johnny Davis (8.0) provided scoring punch, and Corky Calhoun and Robin Jones played excellent defense. Lloyd Neal, hampered by knee problems much of the year, had several great games when he was healthy.

Overall, the Blazers with Walton were, on paper, the most impressive team in the league. Yet sports prognosticators almost unanimously picked Philadelphia, Boston, Los Angeles, and Golden State as the teams to beat. Why not Portland? Three reasons: road record, inexperience, and lingering doubts about health.

First, the road problem. Portland's record away from home was a mediocre 14-27, slightly below the league average. Playoff crowds and pressures intensify the home-court advantage. The 5-12 mark during Walton's absences gave the Blazers only the fourth best overall record in the league. Barring upsets, Portland could not expect to have homecourt advantage past the first round.

Second, inexperience. League observers noted that the Trail Blazers, while 14-1 in games decided by over 20 points, had only a 23-27 record in games decided by under 12 points. Portland won games by getting off to a big start, outscoring opponents 49 times in the first quarters of games and 48 times in second quarters. Analysts suspected the Blazers might fold under the pressure of tight playoff games and hard first-period defense by experienced squads.

Third, injuries. While every member of the 12-man squad was available for playoff duty, not everyone was 100 percent. Walton's ankle remained badly swollen, and he suffered from other assorted aches produced by season-long pounding. Lucas was hampered by a pulled hamstring and Hollins by a bad elbow on his shooting arm. Lloyd Neal, who had knee surgery in training camp, missed February and a week in March, and faced surgery again at the close of the season. Aggravation of the injuries of Walton and Lucas could be fatal to Blazer chances; loss of any other starter or key reserve would be a severe blow.

So on the eve of the playoffs, the Trail Blazers, a talented, deep team who enjoyed the incredibly enthusiastic support of fans who had filled up 98 percent of the available seats throughout the year, were faced with the same task they had faced at the start of the season. Their credentials tarnished by doubts, they had to convince skeptical critics that they had finally arrived. The only place to do that was on the court; the only way was a string of victories leading to the NBA Finals.

4

ROUND ONE:
Portland Trail Blazers
vs.
Chicago Bulls

THE QUESTIONS about the Blazers would be answered in a hurry, as Portland had drawn the toughest of the possible first-round opponents—the red-hot Chicago Bulls. Portland had defeated Chicago in all four meetings this season. But they'd managed to catch the Bulls three times in November and December, when early season problems at one point resulted in a 13-game Chicago losing streak. After the Blazers' last victory, a 90–87 triumph at Chicago, the Bulls had gone on a 20 of 24 tear to wind up the season.

The Bulls' offense was built around the 7'2" 240-pound frame of Artis Gilmore, the first choice in the ABA dispersal draft. Midway through the season, Coach Ed Badger moved Gilmore from the high to the low post, and Artis proceeded to demonstrate why he was a million-dollar property. He led the Bulls in scoring with a variety of high percentage hooks, dunks, and short left-handed bankers. Getting the ball to Artis was primarily the job of Stormin' Norman Van Lier, the emotional heart of the Bulls. Van Lier, one of the premier assist men in basketball (third in

The Pride of Portland

the NBA in 1976–77), created many offensive opportunities with his penetration.

If the ball didn't get into Gilmore and if Van Lier couldn't penetrate, the Bulls were in trouble. A poor shooting team, Chicago had managed only .391 against the Blazers. Forward Mickey Johnson, a budding star who had been drafted and cut by the Blazers in 1974, was the one consistent shooter. Former NCAA player of the year Scott May had helped the Bulls enormously after missing the first two months of the season with mononucleosis, but he still suffered from costly rookie mistakes. Guard Wilbur Holland was a non-passer and notorious streak shooter. Jack Marin, a ten-year veteran, and John Mengelt provided the only punch off the bench.

Defense was the key to the Bulls' success, and the heart was, once again, Gilmore and Van Lier. Artis, fourth in the NBA in rebounding and shot blocking, clogged the middle, intimidating and destroying other teams' patterns. Van Lier, a perennial all-NBA defensive team choice, specialized in harassing point guards and picking up offensive fouls. The rest of the Bulls were less talented, but hardworking, physical defensive players.

For Portland, countering the Bulls' offense meant keeping the ball away from Gilmore. Jack Ramsay assigned Walton to front Gilmore, play him face to face to prevent the pass. If Gilmore did slip away, Lucas would provide help from the weak side. If Gilmore didn't get the ball, Ramsay knew, Chicago's movement would stop, and the Bulls could be pressured into taking poor percentage outside shots.

On offense, the Blazers also had to keep Gilmore away from the basket. Stationing Walton on the high post did take away much of Bill's offense, but it opened the middle for drives by Twardzik and Gross. Walton's scoring slack could be picked up by Lucas. Neither Scott May nor

The Pride of Portland

Mickey Johnson had the size, strength, or experience to counter Maurice, and they had little defensive help on the bench.

As 8:00 P.M. game time at Memorial Coliseum on April 12, 1977, grew near, Ramsay was confident his game plan was sound. But one additional unique element complicated his planning. All but two of the NBA officials had voted to strike the playoffs, sending the league scurrying to find replacements who were inexperienced and prone to err. Ramsay knew that several of his players, especially Walton, had the quickness to make defensive blocks and steals that other players would have to foul to make. If the referees' lack of exposure to these abilities led to foul trouble, the short best-of-three series could easily fall to the Bulls.

The referees' strike also produced the first Walton minicontroversy of the year. In the last game of the season, Walton had remarked to Lucius Allen that he didn't think it was right that the players cross the referees' picket lines. A referee heard the remark and passed it on to some members of the press eager for a new Walton story. The next day, several newspapers trumpeted Walton's supposed boycott of the playoffs.

Walton's new maturity and poise quickly stifled the story, however. He simply announced that, although he had his own opinions, he was simply one member of the NBA Players' Association, and he would abide by their decision to participate in the playoffs. As quickly as it arose, the controversy died, and Walton prepared to concentrate on playing ball once more.

And concentrate he did, right from the first second of the game played in front of 12,774 screaming Blazermaniacs. Jumping against the taller Gilmore, Walton cleanly tipped the ball to Hollins, who fed Lucas for a 15-foot jumper. Swish went the ball, and the Blazers had their first-ever playoff points. Three fast break baskets bracketed a stuff by Gilmore, and the Blazers were off to an 8–2 lead. As the Bulls called a hasty time-out, the cheering fans were sure the Blazers were jumping out to that big early lead so important in their regular season triumphs.

But when the players returned to the court, it soon became apparent that the Blazers had not one, but two, opponents. The inexperienced referees were whistling like sailors on leave. By the 4:30 mark, Walton, who had fouled out of only five of 65 regular season games, had picked up his third foul. Time after time throughout the game, foul calls disrupted the Blazers' momentum, allowing the cold-shooting Bulls to pull close.

Two free throws by Scott May tied the score at 19 with 2:35 to go in the first quarter. Then the Blazers rallied behind Bob Gross to finish the period with a 10–0 spurt that gave them a 29–19 lead.

Early in the second quarter Blazers fans received the scare of their lives. After scoring the first basket of the period, Maurice Lucas pulled up in pain, grabbing his injured hamstring. Trainer Ron Culp hurried him into the locker room. Walton was forced to return to the game, and another quick foul call on him could have crippled the Blazer chances.

But Walton and Gilmore battled each other to a standstill without fouling. The tempo was to the Bulls' liking, and Portland couldn't get the running game going. Only several turnovers and cold shooting prevented Chicago from creeping back to even.

Late in the first half, Lucas returned to the floor amid a giant roar from the crowd. He immediately drilled a 25-foot jumper. Moments later, the Blazers went into the locker room with a 52–42 lead.

The story of the third quarter was the brilliant shooting of Maurice Lucas against the desperate clutch free throw

The Pride of Portland

shooting of the Bulls. In the middle of the period Lucas hit ten straight points. But the Bulls paraded to the line in between baskets by Johnson and Holland that allowed them to whittle the lead to 73–68 at the end of three. Walton had picked up number four after 25 minutes of foulless ball.

The lead stretched to seven in the beginning of the fourth quarter. An enraged Lucas picked up his fourth foul. He charged the terrified, inexperienced referee, grabbing him by the whistle and nearly choking him. An experienced ref would have tossed him from the game, but Walton pulled him away and he escaped with a technical. Moments later, Lucas picked up number five and the Bulls miraculously drew even at 77.

But Jack Ramsay called time out and pulled the Blazers together. The running game that disappeared in the cacophony of whistles in the first quarter suddenly reappeared. Walton fired outlet baskets to Hollins and Gilliam; Lucas hit four crucial buckets. The Bulls managed only six more points. With the hoarse, hysterical crowd on its feet, Corky Calhoun slam-dunked with 16 seconds left to make the final score 96–83. The Blazers were up 1–0.

Jack Ramsay's strategy had worked perfectly. Walton only had 11 points and nine rebounds, but he held big Artis to 13 points. More important, keeping Gilmore away from the basket stopped the Bulls' offensive movement. They shot a miserable .385 from the floor, compared to the Blazers' .530, and they committed 31 costly turnovers. Only 23–27 free throw shooting (the Blazers were 8–10) kept the game close.

The entire starting five for the Blazers had superb games. Lucas hit 14 of 17 shots for 29 points. Gross hit seven for ten, and Dave Twardzik seven for nine. Walton, in addition to his great defense under the incredible stress of three early fouls, dished out assists. Overall, the Blazers outassisted their opponents 28–13 (Van Lier had eight), as the Bulls were reduced to desperate perimeter shooting and one-on-one ball for most of the game.

The first road test came at 7:30 P.M., April 15, in a Chicago Stadium packed with 20,000-plus fans whose deafening roar made Portland Memorial Coliseum seem like a library reference room. The game the Bulls' followers saw was remarkably similar to the first game. Portland outshot Chicago in the first half by a remarkable .600 to .391, but the Bulls managed a 50–46 halftime lead by tripping to the free throw line 19 times to the Blazers' eight. In a controversial fracas, Herm Gilliam was tossed from the game and Maurice Lucas assessed a technical foul in an incident started by a vicious elbow thrown at Gilliam by Wilbur Holland. Gilliam kicked at Holland in return, and Bulls assistant coach Gene Tormohlen rushed onto the court and grabbed Gilliam by the throat. Lucas was forced to come to the rescue, freeing Herm and scaring fans who tried to come onto the court. The referees, possibly intimidated by the huge crowd, ignored Holland's elbow and Tormohlen's charge, and only punished the Blazers. Gilliam's loss was to prove critical in the second half.

The one major difference between the first and second games was that the two talented centers began to get into the offense in the first half. Gilmore, adjusting to Walton's overplaying the hood shot, faked and broke free for layups and dunks. Walton responded to the challenge by outrunning the slower Gilmore on the fast break.

Walton began to outplay Gilmore after intermission as the Blazers forged a 65–60 lead. But in a 35-second stretch Walton picked up his fourth and fifth fouls. With the score 77–76 with one second left in the third, Gilmore drove home a bucket, was fouled, and sunk the free throw for a 79–77 Bull lead.

For the first five minutes of the final stanza the lead see-

The Pride of Portland

sawed back and forth, with neither team managing more than a two-point lead. Portland was hampered by fouls to Twardzik and Hollins, and both eventually fouled out, crippling a guard crew already depleted by the first-half ejection of Gilliam.

Walton banked in a turnaround jumper to give the Blazers their last lead, 90–88. Then Gilmore went to work again, scoring and passing out to red-hot Mickey Johnson and Wilbur Holland. The Bulls controlled the pace with Portland's speed out of the game. With 1:21 left, Chicago had a seemingly insurmountable 105–98 lead.

But the pumped-up, intense Bill Walton refused to concede defeat. A ten-foot jumper from the right baseline made it 105–100. Seconds later, Walton, with exquisite timing, went high to block a Gilmore hook. The resulting fast break resulted in a Lucas lay-in that made the score 105–102.

With eight seconds left, the Blazers stole the ball once again, and a Walton stuff made it 105–104.

But at this point, the comeback was halted by the experience of Norm Van Lier, who had a wonderful 11-assist game. Larry Steele and Johnny Davis trapped Wilbur Holland, but before they could tie him up, Van Lier alertly called time out. With three seconds remaining, Holland was fouled on the inbounds pass, and coolly sunk two free throws for a 107–104. The Windy City went wild, and the teams headed back to Portland for the final shoot-out.

Once again, Portland's percentage was a blistering .580 to the Bulls' .433. Keying the Bulls' victory was their 29–36 performance at the free throw line (the Blazers were a poor 10–20), the scoring of Artis Gilmore (27 points), and the fouling out of Lionel Hollins and Dave Twardzik, who had combined for 40 points.

Game Three was played on Sunday, April 17, in a Memorial Coliseum packed with 12,520 fans who drowned out the public address announcer as Gross, Lucas, Walton, Hollins, and Twardzik were introduced. The homecourt worked its magic again, and the Blazers dominated the first 30 minutes of the game. Gross and Walton hit four field goals apiece in the first quarter to spur a 27–21 Portland lead. Whistles continued to blow in the second quarter, but in this game the fouls were about even. The Blazers managed their second 30-point quarter of the series to take a 57–46 halftime lead. Walton had done a marvelous job, shooting five of eight while limiting Artis Gilmore to a single field goal. Neither Holland, who scored 26 in Game Two, nor Norm Van Lier managed to score a point. The only area of concern was three fouls each on Lucas, Walton, and Twardzik.

Twardzik and Gross were the leaders as Portland, not cooling off during intermission, ran the score to 77–61 with 4:09 remaining in the third. Then, for the first time in the series, the floodgates opened for Chicago, and everything the Bulls tossed up suddenly went in. Before the bewildered Blazers could catch their breath, Chicago had reeled off 14 straight to pull within two, 77–75. Gilliam finally managed a basket and Walton sunk one of two free throws for an 80–75 lead at the end of three.

Once again, as he had so many times during the long season, Jack Ramsay settled his young troops. Aggressive defense triggered a running game in the first five minutes of the final period, and once again the lead was up to 13.

But Blazer fans didn't get much of a chance to settle back. With the score 92–79, Lucas committed his fifth foul, and went to the bench. Taking immediate advantage, the Bulls once more closed in, led by the offense and defense of big Artis Gilmore. Walton committed his fifth foul, and Gilmore made two free throws to make the score 94–90 Portland. Walton countered with a hook, 96–90. Then tragedy struck. A phantom foul was called on Walton as Mickey Johnson drove the lane, and the heart of the Blazer team left the game with six fouls. The crowd leaped to its feet with a prolonged ovation.

Mickey Johnson converted the three-point play to make it 96–93. Then Maurice Lucas, in the quintessential power forward move, backed in against the smaller Johnson to put the Blazers up by five. Van Lier committed a costly offensive foul, then Lucas got the ball to Robin Jones at the top of the key. The poor-shooting reserve center whirled around for a jump shot that touched nothing but net. As the ecstatic Jones hustled down court, he waved clenched fists in the air and the crowd went wild.

But again the Bulls refused to die. John Mengelt, who scored 28 points off the bench, hit two free throws. Richie Powers hit Lucas with a loose-ball call, his sixth foul, and he reluctantly joined Walton and Twardzik on the bench. Gilmore's free throw cut the lead to four, 100–96.

The Coliseum was mass hysteria as Lionel Hollins was called for an offensive foul on the inbounds play. Fifty-eight seconds left. The Bulls called time out, then set up a play that resulted in the veteran Jack Marin hitting a jumper from the foul line: 100–98 with a big 35 seconds left.

This time the Blazers called time to plot their strategy for a play that could end their season if it went wrong. Cool veteran Corky Calhoun inbounded to Gross, and the ball went to Lionel Hollins. Hollins, the goat of just a moment before, dribbled as the 24-second clock wound down. With just four seconds left on the shot clock Lionel accelerated to the top of the key. His jumper went down and the Blazers led by four with just 14 seconds left.

After 143 minutes, 44 seconds of brutal pressure basketball, the gallant Bulls finally succumbed. Four more Blazer free throws made the final 106–98.

The Pride of Portland

Bob Gross's 26 points (ten of 17 from the floor, six of six at the line); Walton's 11 rebounds; and Hollins' nine assists and clutch shot pulled out the incredible victory. The Bulls outrebounded the Blazers by a whopping 42–27, and for the first time in the series outshot them .529 to .500. The Blazers' determination and courage won this game for them. They proved they could survive the pressure of playoff competition.

5

ROUND TWO:
Portland Trail Blazers
vs.
Denver Nuggets

FOR THE BEST-OF-SEVEN second round of the playoffs, the Blazers couldn't have drawn an opponent more different from Chicago than the Denver Nuggets. Denver, led by three-time ABA Coach of the Year Larry Brown, played a game very similar to that of the Blazers: fast break offense; pressure, overplaying defense.

Just how close the teams were was reflected in the results of their regular season series. Each team won two games, each won a game on the other's homecourt. After four games, the teams finished only 12 points, three rebounds, and .008 in shooting percentage apart.

At center for the Nuggets was Dan Issel, six-year veteran from the University of Kentucky who had been the starting Western Conference center in the 1976–77 All-Star Game. Issel's forte was perimeter shooting, "Issel Missiles" tossed up from as far as 20 feet. He was mobile, a good passer, and finished tenth in the NBA in scoring with 22.3 per game.

If Issel was the star, David Thompson was the Nugget's superstar. He was College Player of the Year in 1974 when he led North Carolina State to the NCAA title, beating Walton's UCLA team in the semis and Maurice Lucas' Marquette Warriors in the final. A number one draft choice of both the NBA and ABA, playing mostly at forward because of his super leaping ability, Thompson finished fourth in the league in scoring (25.9).

The other forward was all-league defensive player Bobby Jones, now a 76er. The Seagrams All-Star Award computer selected the 6'9" Jones as the best all-around player in the league for 1976–77. Jones was third in the league in field goal percentage (.570), sixth in steals (2.27), averaged 15.1 points per game, and ranked among the forward leaders in assists and rebounds. Another great jumper.

Three much-traveled ballplayers shared the bulk of the playing time at guard: 6'3" Ted (Hound Dog) McClain, a teammate of Blazer Lloyd Neal at Tennessee State, was a fine penetrator but a spotty outside shooter; 6' 3" Jim Price, who had begun the season with Milwaukee, went to Buffalo, then ended up starting for the Nuggets, was a fine defensive player and excellent passer; 6' Mack Calvin, a seven-year veteran who was back with Denver after stints with three other teams in two years, had scored 26 points in the final game of the regular season against Portland. Like the other two guards, Mack loved to run.

Leading the front court reserves was 12-year veteran Paul Silas—playoff-seasoned, a rugged defender, the best offensive rebounder in basketball. Veteran Willie Wise, 6'6", was a fine outside shooter who had averaged over 20 ppg four consecutive years in the ABA. Giant 7'1" second-year man Marvin Webster and nine-year veteran Byron Beck spelled Issel.

Offensively, Denver's weakness was outside shooting. To beat the Nuggets, the Blazers felt that they had to have Walton clogging the middle, shutting off the penetration

The Pride of Portland

of Thompson and the guards and keeping Jones off the offensive boards. If Issel got hot, Lucas would have to switch over to cover him.

In regard to the Portland offense, Jack Ramsay felt the Blazers could outrun Denver. Walton was quicker than Issel, and Hollins, Twardzik, and Davis were younger and faster than Denver's veteran crew. But the Blazers had to be particularly careful to get back when a guard penetrated on offense, to prevent Denver from running two-on-one or three-on-one fast breaks.

With the teams so close in ability, Portland's biggest enemy could well be Denver's homecourt advantage. The first game of the series was absolutely critical. A Portland victory in the mile-high city would shift the advantage to the Blazers.

Denver coach Larry Brown was just as determined not to let the homecourt advantage slip away. To counteract Maurice Lucas, who had averaged 23.5 points and 13 rebounds against Denver during the regular season, Brown started the cagey veteran Paul Silas at power forward. David Thompson moved to guard, where Brown hoped he could operate more effectively against the smaller Portland guards. Dan Issel was instructed to stay on the perimeter, with the hope that he could draw Walton away from the basket to open the middle for Bobby Jones and Ted McClain.

Denver's execution was nearly perfect in the opening minutes of Game One. Before 17,995 fans crammed into McNichols Sports Arena, the Nuggets scored the first three baskets en route to a 16–8 bulge. Dan Issel hit five uncontested 20-to-25-foot shots and Paul Silas snagged a couple key offensive rebounds.

But the Blazers, demonstrating the maturity they found in the Chicago series, refused to depart from their game plan. Increasing the defensive pressure and looking for fast break opportunities, they drew back to tie at 21. A Willie Wise jumper gave the Nuggets a slender 25–23 lead at the end of one period.

The second quarter belonged to Portland. The Blazer strategy of forcing Denver outside began to work, as Issel cooled off. Gross and Twardzik penetrated with abandon, and, drawing fouls, gave them the chance to go 18 for 19 at the foul line for the game. Lucas drilled four jumpers as the Trail Blazers went into the locker room with a 50–45 edge.

The old sports cliché "When the going gets tough, the tough get going" proved true after the intermission. Both teams realized that this first game was the key to the series. The second half of this tension-filled game was dominated by the superstars of each team.

The third period belonged to Bill Walton. After a 12–6 opening spurt put Denver ahead by one, the big center went to work. He slammed home an Alley Oop pass from Gross, then went on to drop in nine more third-period points. At the end of three, the visitors led by six.

But David Thompson wouldn't let Denver lay down and die. Showing the incredible speed, grace, and leaping ability that would win him a record $4-million contract the next year, "Black Magic" keyed a 10–0 burst to open the fourth quarter. Suddenly, Denver had an 81–77 advantage.

With three minutes left, Denver clung to a three-point lead. But Dave Twardzik, with the kind of twisting drive that made him such a factor in the Chicago series, drew Bobby Jones's sixth personal foul. Denver's best defensive player was forced to exit, the Twardzik's two free throws drew them within one.

Seconds later, Walton grabbed his own rebound and scored to give the Blazers the lead. Denver responded with two quick buckets. With 1:23 left, Herm Gilliam fouled

The Pride of Portland

David Thompson in the act of shooting. It looked like the game was over.

But in this showdown before the screaming Denver crowd, it was David Thompson who folded under pressure. He missed both free throws, and Twardzik drove the lane once more to put Portland within one. The Nuggets moved the ball up court, hoping for a basket that would put the game out of reach. But Thompson whipped a pass out of bounds. Blazer ball.

Here the script called for a superstar once more, and this time Maurice Lucas responded with a bucket that gave the Blazers the lead with 34 seconds left. David Thompson once again took the ball. Fouled by Lionel Hollins, this time he dropped both charity tosses to put the Nuggets back on top.

Portland called a time-out with 20 seconds left. Ramsay, surrounded by his exhausted troops, outlined a play. The ball was to be inbounded to Lucas, who would feed the ball to Dave Twardzik cutting back door. The buzzer sounded and the teams took the floor. The ball was indeed tossed to Lucas at the top of the key. But Luke never even glanced at Twardzik. As the clock ticked away, he backed Dan Issel toward the basket in a fierce confrontation. With eleven seconds left, he turned and shot. The 14-foot line drive jumper rocketed through the hoop. Tight Portland defense forced a desperate miss by Hound Dog McClain, Walton grabbed the rebound, and Portland won 101–100 in perhaps the most exciting game in the history of the franchise.

After the game, in an uproarious Portland locker room, reporters crowded around Maurice Lucas. "I wanted that shot. It was a pressure situation and I really wanted it." Suddenly, Jack Ramsay quieted the crowd for what appeared to be some serious comments on the game. He

The Pride of Portland

started, "First, Luke gets fined fifty dollars for not running the play." The Blazers broke up in hysterical laughter as the jubilation continued. The home advantage had now fallen to them.

Portland's momentum continued into the second game, played on April 22 at 9:30 P.M. .740 shooting carried the Blazers to a 30–24 first-period lead. Maurice Lucas continued his brilliant playing, hitting seven of eight from the floor on the way to 16 first-half points. But Dan Issel was just as hot for Denver, hitting for 17 to give Denver a 52–51 halftime lead.

The Blazers continued to move and shoot extraordinarily well in the second half. But they finally succumbed to an old enemy that wreaked so much havoc in the first two Chicago games—the inexperienced referees. For the game, Denver shot 39 free throws to the Blazers' 15; they converted 31 to 12 for Portland. The Nuggets shot ten free throws to none for Portland in the third quarter, but the Blazers hung close.

When Bill Walton, who had 19 points, 16 rebounds, and ten assists, fouled out with 7:36 to go, Denver gradually pulled away. Walton was so furious that he stood in front of the Blazer bench for the last seven minutes, despite the hooting and screaming of the Denver fans. Ramsay was so upset he had to be restrained from charging the referees after the game. Despite hitting 60 percent from the floor, the Blazers fell 121–110. After the game, even Denver coach Larry Brown admitted that the loss of Walton on fouls was the key to his team's victory: "Losing Walton at the end hurt Portland. I've never seen a player who was more crucial to his team's success than Walton. He can do anything his team needs—pass, rebound, shoot, play defense, give leadership, and he fires the outlet pass quicker and more accurately than anyone I've ever seen play the game."

The Pride of Portland

The second loss did not overshadow the fact that Portland had accomplished its primary objective: capturing one vital game in enemy territory. The Blazers moved back to the friendly confines of Memorial Coliseum with the chance to take command of the series.

On Sunday, April 24, before 12,736 Blazermaniacs, the crucial Game Three began. But it was Denver who came out fighting, as they sprinted to a 10–3 lead. Ramsay quickly called time out to remind his team that they were finally back at home, and the Blazers responded with their own 11–0 spurt to go out in front 14–10.

Maurice Lucas continued his series-long brilliant shooting in the first half, throwing down 17 first-half points. Walton added 12, taking advantage of the fact that Dan Issel was hobbled by an injured toe. Only the magic of David Thompson kept the Nuggets within six at the half. By intermission, the 6'4" leaper from North Carolina State had hit nine of 15 from the floor and three of three from the line for 21 points.

Denver struggled back in the third quarter. Bobby Jones had come alive, Dan Issel rallied from a shooting slump to hit a couple key buckets, and Thompson remained hot. Only a launch-and-pray running two-hander from midcourt by Hollins gave the Blazers an 81–80 lead at the end of three.

Portland fans were anxious as the fourth quarter began. Maurice Lucas, whose play had been so vital, went to the bench with five fouls. The rest of the starters were tired by the incredible pressure and pace of the frenetic play. But once again, as they had so many times that season, the Portland bench responded. Although hampered by his injured knee, Lloyd Neal came in to grab an incredible nine rebounds in just seven minutes of playing time. Robin Jones snared three rebounds and hit two of three from the floor in his nine minutes. Herm Gilliam and Wally Walker played with equal intensity. Although Lucas fouled out with 4:21 left, the Blazers moved to a 107–100 lead with a little more than a minute left.

But the game was not yet in hand. David Thompson threw down two quick baskets, and McClain converted a pass from Jim Price to make it 107–106 with 22 seconds left. Price fouled Gilliam intentionally with 15 seconds left. In a situation the reverse of Game One, Herm went to the line with the chance to convert two free throws to put the game out of reach. But the pressure got to him as it got to Thompson in Game One. He made the first, but the second bounced off the rim to Issel. A quick outlet pass went to McClain, who dashed off to a speeding Jim Price as the Nuggets had a three-on-one break that could tie the game.

But the monkey once more ended up on Denver's back. As the crowd held its breath, Price fumbled the ball. Bill Walton alertly picked it up and fired up court to Twardzik for the clinching basket. The Blazers won 110–106.

In the two critical games of the series, the Trail Blazers had reached the crucial break in the last seconds. But it wasn't luck. Rather, the Portland team that had won only 23 of 50 games decided by under 12 points had come of age. The Denver Nuggets, who had a 4–14 record in games decided by under five points during the regular season, had not been able to rise to the challenge.

Denver's back was against the wall in Game Four, played on April 26. "We've never played a bigger game," said Larry Brown, as he desperately sought to rally the spirits of his squad.

But the Nuggets played like a demoralized team, and Portland rolled to a 32–24 first-quarter lead. Dan Issel, still hobbled by that badly infected toe, was missing from the outside, allowing Walton to clog the middle. David Thompson, who had received a standing ovation from the

The Pride of Portland

record 12,930 Portland crowd, raged furiously at two early questionable foul calls. Portland had been the victim of these kinds of calls in Game Two, but had managed to retain their intensity. But in this game Thompson lost his concentration, and he managed only seven field goals and 16 points, 24 points below his Game Three mark.

Only Mack Calvin kept Denver close. In just 21 minutes of playing time, the 6 veteran, who was playing for his seventh professional team, tossed in eight of ten from the field and 12 of 13 free throws. He almost singlehandedly brought the Nuggets within two, 78–76, at the end of the third quarter.

In the fourth quarter, however, the hero of the game, Bob Gross, took over once more. Gross had hit for 12 in the first half, and he added 12 more in the fourth to give the Blazers a 105–96 win. At one point, Gross was so hot he tossed a 25-foot Alley Oop pass to Walton that hit off the board and snuggled into the net. Throughout the series, Gross had played extraordinarily well. With help from Walton, he had stopped the penetration of Bobby Jones, and kept him off the boards. On offense, his perfect execution of Blazer plays and his speed on the break allowed him to elude the best defense forward in basketball for 63 points. Said Jack Ramsay of Gross's performance in Game Four, "Bobby played the best game I've ever seen him play and one of the finest games a small forward has played in the league all season. His defense was excellent, he moved well, and he shot well."

Due to television scheduling, the Denver Nuggets had five days to regroup before Game Five, and Larry Brown made a number of changes in his game plan. He decided to move David Thompson back to forward, where he hoped his quickness and leaping ability would overwhelm Bob Gross. With Gross neutralized, guards Calvin and Price would fall back and help Jones and Issel collapse on Walton and Lucas. Denver was determined to make the Portland guards hit from the outside to win.

The Denver strategy worked perfectly in the first half. Dan Issel, recovered from his toe infection, played the kind of game he had in Denver's previous victory. David Thompson went over, under, around, and through Bob Gross for 18 first-half points. For the Blazers, Lucas managed 12 points, but only two rebounds in the half. With the offense slowed by the lack of penetration, Portland took poor percentage shots.

The situation grew even more serious in the third quarter as Denver increased their six-point halftime lead to 12. Worse, Dave Twardzik, whose defense and driving had sparked the Blazers repeatedly, was carried from the court with a badly injured ankle. Only ferocious play by Maurice Lucas, who pulled down eight third-quarter rebounds, kept the Blazers within six at the end of the period.

Walton opened the fourth period by blocking a Dan Issel shot, and the play of the big redhead once again seemed to rally his team. Suddenly, the Nuggets' shooting cooled off. David Thompson, who had 27 points at the end of three, managed only two more baskets. Courageous play by Herm Gilliam, Bob Gross, Lionel Hollins, Lucas, and Walton brought the Blazers within one, 97–96.

Marvin Webster, 7'1", whose inspired play (ten points, ten rebounds) had been instrumental in the Denver lead, responded with two free throws to make it 99–96 with 1:56 left. Webster scurried back on defense to block a shot by Hollins, who had begun to get hot. The teams traded buckets before Walton hit a free throw to shave the lead to two.

Jim Price, whose miscue allowed Portland to clinch Game Three, had responded to his starting asignment in this game by triggering the Denver offense with 11 assists.

The Pride of Portland

But with the game on the line, he tried to do it himself, driving down the middle. Walton came over, leaping high in the air to intimidate the 6'3" guard, and the ball careened off the rim. Then on a break, with 28 seconds left, Lionel Hollins laid the ball in for a 101 tie.

It looked like the Nuggets were folding under pressure one more time, as the Blazers got the ball back with seven seconds left. Walton set a screen for Hollins, but this time his 18-foot jumper missed and the game was sent into overtime.

Unfortunately, the overtime was no contest. David Thompson hit the opening bucket, and Dan Issel tossed in nine overtime points. With Walton and Gross having fouled out, the Blazers couldn't retaliate. Denver had a 114–105 win, and the series went back to Portland. Said a weary Larry Brown, "Maybe we've got something left."

With less than 24 hours before Game Six, Jack Ramsay was faced with a crucial decision. Dave Twardzik was unable to play. To counteract the Game Five Denver strategy of collapsing on the big men, Ramsay had to make the right choice for the starting assignment, or the Blazers could find themselves flying back to Denver with the series tied.

Ramsay's instincts were to go with the veteran Larry Steele, who had his best year in 1976–77. But Bill Walton and assistant coach Jack McKinney lobbied for Johnny Davis. The lightning-quick 6'2" rookie from Dayton had been used sparingly in the last month of the season, and had seen only 59 minutes of playoff time. But Walton felt that Davis' speed made him impossible to cover on the press. McKinney argued that the best way to beat a collapsing defense was a sizzling fast break that didn't give the defense time to set. In a move that demonstrated Ramsay's character and the respect he accorded to his assistant and captain, Ramsay gave the nod to Johnny Davis.

The Pride of Portland

The decision to start Davis may have been Ramsay's best of the year. Before 12,924 fans, who were on their feet before the opening tap, Lucas opened the game with a two-handed stuff. The Blazers were running the fast break with a vengeance, catapulting to a 24–10 lead. Larry Brown called time out and set up a full court press. But the quicksilver Davis cut through the press time after time like a hot knife through butter. By the time the first-period buzzer sounded, Portland had a 33–16 lead.

The Blazers never looked back as they breezed to their first playoff romp 108–92. The outmanned bewildered Nuggets shot 42 percent from the field, and a miserable 24 of 47 from the free throw line. Issel and Jones only managed four field goals apiece. David Thompson was a paltry six for 14 from the field and five for 12 from the free throw line. Only Marvin Webster's 16 rebounds and 13 points prevented complete humiliation.

Portland, on the other hand, played a marvelous team game. Johnny Davis, rising to the challenge, played 39 minutes, hit ten of 14 from the field, five of seven from the line, and had four steals. Walton had 12 rebounds and nine assists. Hollins tossed in 21 and Larry Steele 14 in just 21 minutes. Even substitute center Robin Jones chipped in with four of five shooting from the floor. At the end of the game, the fans had gone wild, and an ecstatic Jack Ramsay, waving his sport jacket in the air like a victory trophy, looked forward to the Western Conference Championship Series.

6

ROUND THREE:
Portland Trail Blazers
vs.
Los Angeles Lakers

*T*HE BLAZERS HAD TO WAIT until May 4 to find out who their next opponents would be: The Division-winning Los Angeles Lakers or the Golden State Warriors. Portland players and coaching staff believed that they would have won the Division if it hadn't been for Walton's injuries. They hoped the Lakers would best the Warriors to prove their superiority where it counted—on the court.

The 53 victories—highest total in the NBA—compiled by the Lakers was a magnificent achievement for a team not significantly changed from the 40–42 fourth-place club of 1975–76. The primary reason for the second (after the Blazers') most miraculous rise in the NBA was their new coach, Jerry West.

After a brilliant college career at West Virginia, West joined the Lakers in 1960. His subsequent career made him a choice on virtually everyone's all-time all-NBA squad. Perhaps the best guard in NBA history, West had every asset one could ask of a player—quickness, agility, great shooting touch, superb defense, extraordinary basketball intelligence, and, most of all, a fierce determination to win.

He was an inspirational player who had led his 1972–73 Lakers to an NBA crown.

West carried his determination, intelligence, and inspirational ability into coaching. After making the unusual move of hiring an assistant to handle the offense and one to handle the defense (Stan Albrecht and former Blazer head coach [1972–73] Jack McClosky), West devoted himself to developing the kind of coordinated, detailed game plans so necessary for a successful professional basketball team. His fair, knowledgeable, enthusiastic manner boosted the spirits of his team and led to their tremendous season.

Especially uplifted by West's presence was the great center Kareem Abdul-Jabbar, who played with the intensity and enthusiasm of a rookie. The Lakers were a team built around this one man, and their success reflected his fantastic season: third in the NBA in scoring (26.2); first in field goal percentage (.579); second in rebounding to Walton (13.3); second in blocked shots to Walton (3.18). A rugged, durable player despite his seemingly slender frame, Jabbar started all 82 Laker games for the second year in a row.

West had gotten the maximum from Jabbar's supporting cast. The second leading scorer was veteran forward Cazzie Russell, a superb jump-shooter who raised his average from 11.8 to 16.4 points per game. For most of the year, Russell's front court mate had been power forward Kermit Washington, a rugged 6'8", 230-pound four-year veteran from American University. Washington's bone-crunching defense and rebounding had taken a lot of pressure off Kareem. But Washington was forced out of the playoffs by a knee injury, a bad blow to the lakers.

With Washington out, West was forced to go with low-scoring, unheralded Don Ford, a 6'9", 215-pound second-year man from University of California at Santa Barbara. Ford had yet to prove himself as a rebounder or a defender. Backing up at the forward spots were 6'9" veteran Cornell Warner, a nonscorer, and rookie Tom Abernathy, 6'7", a former starting forward on the 1976 NCAA Championship Indiana University team.

Third leading scorer was guard Lucius Allen, who had come to the Lakers from Milwaukee in the middle of the 1974-75 season (for Jim Price, who later ended up at Denver). Allen averaged 14.6 points per game, led the Lakers in assists, and provided the only backcourt quickness.

Starting at the other guard was defensive specialist Don ("Duck") Chaney, picked up as a free agent after St. Louis of the ABA folded. Chaney had been a key player on several championship Celtic teams.

Backing up at guard were Earl Tatum, a 6'4" high-leaping rookie from Marquette University, and much-traveled (seven teams in six years) Johnny Neumann, a 6'6" guard with a good outside shot.

The focal point for the lion's share of the publicity about this Western Conference Championship Series was the battle of the two former UCLA centers. The rivalry was built up as a new duel reminiscent of the titanic Russell-Chamberlain confrontations of old.

Neither Walton nor Abdul-Jabbar could be drawn into a heated discussion of his rival. Said Walton: "It's no big deal . . . I'm excited. As Kareem gets older, he gets smarter. Physically he's in his prime. I think he's playing the best of his life." Abdul-Jabbar was quoted as saying, "Walton believes in his talent. He tests his skill rather than using muscle to hang on me. It's a challenge to play against a guy this good, on a level above what I go through most nights. It's not so much even winning. It's expressing yourself."

There was, however, a good deal more feeling in both men than showed in their public comments. Walton desperately wanted to outduel Kareem in the spotlight to finally bury the image of his early humiliation by

Abdul-Jabbar in his rookie year. Kareem had shown how intensely he felt about the rivalry by his incredibly intense, goggleless play in LA's 115–111 overtime win at Portland on December 18, five days after *Sports Illustrated* had lauded Walton as the new "King of the Mountain." That game was the only home game Portland lost all season in which Walton was 100 percent healthy.

Walton had a statistical edge in the regular season meetings, scoring 24.3 to Kareem's 25.0, but outrebounding him per game 21 to 13.2, outassisting him 5.0 to 2.7. But LA had managed to win two of the three games in which Walton played.

That last statistic made a telling point ignored by many members of the press. The Walton-Jabbar confrontation was a display of basketball at its peak, a clash of the two most dominant players in the game that would provide countless thrills to basketball fans. But basketball is a team game. Unless one of the big centers managed to significantly dominate the other, the series would be decided in the far less glamorous match-ups of the other four men on the floor. And in these match-ups Portland had significant advantages.

One big advantage was at power forward. With Kermit Washington out for the series, West was forced to go with inexperienced Don Ford. Maurice Lucas was far stronger and far more experienced than the blond second-year man. Lucas should be able to dominate Ford even more than he dominated the Chicago forwards. Since Ford was not a significant offensive threat, Lucas would be free to help out Walton on defense.

The second big advantage was at guard. Lucius Allen dislocated his toe in the Golden State series, and would be out for at least the first two Portland games. Without Allen, the Laker guards were no match for the quickness of

The Pride of Portland

Hollins and Johnny Davis. Allen was also LA's only superior ball handler and assist man.

The third advantage was the grueling seven-game series with Golden State that Los Angeles had just survived. The Lakers, less deep than Portland even with a healthy Washington and Allen, were a tired team with only one day off to rest before Game One.

Jack Ramsay established his game plan for this series based on two objectives: neutralizing Abdul-Jabbar and exploiting the Lakers' weaknesses. Offensively, this meant the fast break: getting the ball down court ahead of Kareem; outrunning the Laker guards; tiring out the team. If the Blazers did have to set up, they would concentrate on creating good movement that would exploit the advantage of Lucas over Ford, exploit the quickness of the Portland guards; and try to get Kareem in foul trouble.

The Lakers, not a good running club, ran a set offense that revolved around Kareem. Walton would front Jabbar, trying to deny him the ball and overplaying his favored sky hook. Since Kareem liked to set up on the left side of the lane, the Blazers would attempt to force the ball to the right. Finally, given the weak ball handling of the Laker guards, Portland would attempt to force turnovers by picking up at half court and applying pressure defense.

The game plan worked to perfection in the critical opening game of the series, played May 6 in the Los Angeles Forum. The Lakers played like a tired ball club. Kareem, who had scored 36 points two nights before in leading his team to the clinching 97–84 win over Golden State, looked lethargic as Portland opened with a 12–2 spurt. West hurriedly called time out with just 3:07 played, but after the break Walton came out to take the play to his rival. The big redhead scored nine points to Kareem's two as the Blazers took a 33–22 lead at the end of

The Pride of Portland

one. Hollins had ten points in the period, and Johnny Davis tossed in a 47-foot heave at the buzzer.

Kareem's play picked up in the second quarter as he began to play Walton even. But the rest of the Lakers were no match for the inspired, fast-breaking Blazers who roared to a 61–43 halftime lead. At the intermission, Lucas had 14 points and nine rebounds. Portland outshot LA .581 to .383, outassisted them 17 to nine.

The rest at halftime did the Lakers some good. Rookie Earl Tatum, who had started in place of Allen, got red hot, taking some of the pressure off Kareem. The Blazers' shooting tailed off as LA began to control the pace, and they closed to within seven, 99–92, early in the fourth quarter. But they weren't able to get any closer. Johnny Davis flew through the Lakers' full court press, setting up offensive opportunities. With 1:15 left, Jerry West took Kareem out of the game, and the final read Portland 121–109. The victory broke LA's 14 consecutive home game win streak.

The starters scored 107 of Portland's 121 points. Maurice Lucas destroyed Don Ford, outscoring him 28 (on 11 for 15 from the floor, six of six at the line) to ten and outrebounding him 15 to three. Walton had 22 points, 13 rebounds, and six assists. Hollins and Davis ran rings around the bewildered LA guards, throwing in 25 and 20 respectively. Bob Gross and Larry Steele held Cazzie Russell to just four for 12 shooting from the field. Kareem Abdul-Jabbar did rally from his horrible first quarter to toss in 30 points. But he only managed ten rebounds and five assists, and the Blazers got up the floor so quickly on offense Kareem didn't block a single shot.

Jerry West, disgruntled by the television scheduling that didn't allow his team adequate rest, summed up the game: "We don't want them to score 121 points against us. They are a lot quicker than we are. I don't know how many bas-

The Pride of Portland

kets they got from four or five feet [it was an astounding 25], but it was quite a few. We can play a lot better than we did."

And play better they did, in the "must-win" second game at the Forum on Sunday, May 8. The Lakers decided to clog the middle to shut down Walton, Lucas, and Gross, preferring to let the guards fire away from the outside. Aggressive offensive rebounding and better shot selection would cut down Portland's fast break opportunities. Finally, Kareem had gotten some badly needed rest, and the Lakers were determined to get the ball to him.

Led by Kareem, the Lakers did shut down Portland's inside game in the first half. Offensively, the 7'3" center was magnificent, hitting 11 of 14 shots on the way to 24 first-half points. Walton was completely taken out of the offense, and Lucas hit only two of eight shots and snared only three rebounds.

But a tremendous performance by Lionel Hollins led the Blazers to a 54–51 halftime lead. Portland's fast break never got rolling, and the clogging of the middle took Johnny Davis' offense away. So the heady 6'3" guard from Arizona State took over. He hit ten of 13 from the floor and four of six from the line to match Kareem's 24 first-half points.

Unfortunately, the intermission cooled down Lionel but didn't slow down Abdul-Jabbar a bit. Kareem opened the third period with a sky hook, triggering a seven-minute LA spurt that put them in front by nine. With the front line of Portland still unable to get untracked, the Blazers' offense had stopped and they looked to be in serious trouble.

But, as had happened so many times during the season and playoffs, Jack Ramsay made the perfect substitution. Into the game came Herm Gilliam, the most veteran of the Blazers and the only man with NBA playoff experience. The "Trickster" immediately hit the last shot of the third quarter to bring Portland within seven, 77–70. Early in the fourth quarter, Kareem came back into the game, but Gilliam stayed hot to keep the Blazers within striking distance. With the score 91–84, Herm went wild. He hit a 20-foot jumper, then added three more in succession. Only two free throws by Abdul-Jabbar kept the Lakers up by one.

The game headed down to the wire. Pressure by Walton forced Kareem to miss a sky hook. Bill hustled down the court, faking Kareem and hitting a short jumper. Two free throws by Don Ford put LA back in front. Hollins broke free for a layup, but Kareem countered with a stuff. LA still led by one, 97–96.

One final time Gilliam came to the rescue. With one minute left, he took a pass, faked once, cut across the lane, and scooped up the ball with his right hand. The incredible driving shot put the Blazers ahead 98–97. Portland got the ball back, but Lionel Hollins was only able to convert one of two at the line. The Lakers called time out with 11 seconds left to plot strategy.

Jack Ramsay and the Blazers had no doubt what that strategy was going to be. The inbound pass went to Abdul-Jabbar, but four Portland players surrounded him. Kareem was forced to take a wild turnaround jump shot that missed by a mile. The buzzer sounded, giving Portland a 99–97 win. Unbelievably, the young Blazers twice defeated a veteran team that had won 38 of 42 home games during the regular season.

After the game, reporters flocked around hero Herm Gilliam, who explained his success: "They were blocking our inside movement. I knew the only way to get back was to start hitting from the outside. I like that kind of situation. My style is more one-on-one and I was able to make the difference. I guess some people think I shouldn't have taken some of those shots. But that's my rhythm. I like to

The Pride of Portland

shoot that way. I'll tell you though, if I had missed a couple of them, I would have been right back on the bench."

Gilliam (24) and Hollins (31) accounted for 55 of Portland's 99 points. Lucas was held to 16 points on six of 18 shooting, and Gross could only manage nine. Walton matched Kareem's 17 rebounds, but his scoring fell to 14.

Abdul-Jabbar, in an incredible performance, hit 17 of 23 field goals and six of nine from the line for 40 points. He added 17 rebounds. Cazzie Russell contributed 21. But Earl Tatum, who hit for 32 in Game One, shot a miserable four for 15, and the rest of the Laker backcourt (Chaney, Johnny Neumann, and Bo Lamar) scraped together 12 points between them.

Three thousand wildly cheering fans crowded the Portland airport when the Blazers returned from their triumphant two games in Los Angeles, and 12,926 jammed Memorial Coliseum for Game Three on Tuesday night, May 10.

The Blazers responded to their return with a blistering first quarter. Establishing the fast tempo they'd lost somewhere in Game One, Portland got inside for 14 of 19, .737 shooting. Lucas and Hollins led the way with ten apiece. The Lakers, relying primarily on perimeter shooting, hit a very respectable 13–22, .591, but they found themselves down 36–29 at the end of one.

Unfortunately, as soon as the second period started, the Lakers abruptly shut down the Portland offense once more. After 36 first-quarter points, the Blazers managed only a combined total of 37 in the second and third quarters.

The Lakers seemed inspired by the return of guard Lucius Allen, whose ball handling and passing created more movement in the LA offense. Abdul-Jabbar, after 70 points in the first two games, concentrated on passing and defense. With several Portland players suffering from a

The Pride of Portland

mild flu (Walton, Lucas, Gross, Hollins, Steele), the Lakers wore them down. LA outscored the Blazers 16–5 in the last five minutes of the second period to cut the Portland lead to one at the half, 54–53.

The Lakers forged into the lead in a very physical third quarter. Herm Gilliam came off the bench and his shooting kept the Blazers within two at the end of the third stanza. With nine minutes left in the game, LA was up by four, 87–77.

The next five minutes were the most spectacular of the playoffs, and perhaps the most awesome performance seen in the NBA in years. Bill Walton returned to the floor with a look of such intensity it reminded observers of his magnificent 21 of 22 shooting against Memphis State in the 1973 NCAA finals.

Walton started his sensational tear with a mid-key jumper. A minute later he stuffed a rebound to tie the game at 81. After Gross tipped in a missed Lucas shot, Walton hit another jumper. Portland led by four. The crowd, sensing Walton's intensity, started to go wild.

The Memorial Coliseum exploded on the next play, one Portland fans will talk about for years. Lucas missed a jumper, got his own rebound, then passed to Walton in the foul circle. Walton roared down the lane, leaped into the air, and rammed in a savage stuff right in the face of his rival, Kareem Abdul-Jabbar. As the smoke cleared, Walton was waving his fists in the air and the Lakers looked completely lost. Said Herm Gilliam, "I wish I had been on the bench, not in the game. I wanted to jump up, do handstands. Bill got that look that says he's handling the case. That look is scary."

After a Laker time-out, Walton came back with three more baskets to make the score 93–84 with 3:42 left in the game. The magnificent center had scored 14 of his team's last 16 points, singlehandedly rallying his team, changing the entire course of the game.

The courageous Kareem didn't quit. He scored, and the Lakers attempted to fight back. But baskets by Hollins and Lucas, plus four free throws, held LA off. Portland, winning 102–97, had taken a 3–0 lead against the team with the best regular season record in the NBA.

After the game, Ramsay talked about Walton's play: "I know it seems as if we went away from our team offense again. But all his shots were out of set plays. If a player on our team started to make shots that were not in our offense, it would throw our whole game off.

"Bill said at halftime that he'd have to go to the basket more. When he gets that look in his face, he's there."

After scoring only eight points in the first 39 minutes, Walton finished with a team-high 22. He added 15 rebounds and nine assists. Lucas recovered a bit from his poor shooting game to tie Walton with 22, and Luke pulled down 11 boards. Herm Gilliam continued his hot shooting, hitting six of nine along with two of two from the line for 14 points.

Walton's heroics tended to overshadow yet another tremendous game by Kareem. While only scoring 21 points, Abdul-Jabbar had 20 rebounds, seven assists, and eight blocked shots. Lucius Allen returned with 14 points and six assists, and rookie Tom Abernathy responded to the playoff pressure with 16 points and five rebounds in a very solid 31 minutes.

Portland's lead in the series seemed insurmountable, but one more victory on the floor was needed to send the unheralded and underdog Blazers into the finals of the NBA Championship.

Game Four began at 8:00 P.M. on Friday, May 13, and the 12,904 Blazermaniacs, who raised a deafening din as

The Pride of Portland

the Portland team was introduced, hoped the date wouldn't be unlucky. They weren't disappointed as the Blazers forged a 31–25 first-period lead. Once again, the series settled down to a contest between Kareem Abdul-Jabbar and the Portland team. Kareem had 13 points, but Portland outrebounded their opponents 14–9 to key the fast break.

The lead was lengthened to ten, 43–33, before the defense tightened. Johnny Neumann came off the bench to score three baskets that narrowed Portland's advantage to one, before a 20-footer at the buzzer gave the Blazers a 49–44 halftime lead.

LA forged ahead in a very physical third quarter, led once again by Kareen and Lucius Allen. Maurice Lucas, once again dominating Don Ford, kept the Blazers close.

Then with 3:30 to go in the third, the break of the game occurred. Kareem Abdul-Jabbar picked up his fifth personal foul, and he was forced to go to the bench. The Blazers quickly took advantage of his absence to toss in nine points to take a 79–73 lead.

Kareem came back in to start the fourth quarter, but his foul trouble limited his aggressiveness on defense. Portland exploited the advantage by driving down the middle. Johnny Davis, invisible in Games Two and Three after the brilliant last game against Denver and the first game versus LA, had returned to life with nine for 12 shooting.

But no Division Championship team dies without a last fight. Abdul-Jabbar and Cazzie Russell led LA back from ten down to close within two, 87–85. Then, as he did in Game One, Maurice Lucas took over. He came off the bench to make it 89–85. Moments later two more jumpers stretched the Portland lead to eight, 93–85. LA closed within four, then another Lucas shot made it 95–89. Moments later, a steal and solo stuff by Johnny Davis made the score 103–93. A final tip-in by Luke with :58 left iced

The Pride of Portland

the 105–101 win. *The Blazers were the 1977 Western Conference Champions.*

High scorer for the Blazers was Lucas, with 26 (18 in the second half). Davis added 21, Walton 19, and Hollins 18. For the Lakers Kareem threw in 30 along with 17 rebounds. Lucius Allen hit for 20 despite the pain of his dislocated toe.

After the game, Lucas talked about his performance down the stretch: "It seemed like everybody on the team wanted the ball down the stretch, but I found myself open quite a bit and I just put it up. Actually, I don't remember who was playing me at the time. I came across a couple of picks that Bill gave me and everything went in."

The play of Lucas was one of the key elements in this unbelievable 4–0 crushing. Lucas outscored Don Ford 92–41, outrebounded him 47–11, and even outassisted him 18–12.

A second key to the win was, as Ramsay expected, the dominance of the Portland guards. Holland and Davis combined for 45 points in Game One and 39 in Game Four. Gilliam hit 24 off the bench to win Game Two. Sixteen steals by the Blazers contributed mightily to the Game Three Portland win. Said Jerry West, "That was the whole difference. Their quickness. Kareem did everything humanly possible to win a basketball game, but we couldn't give him the help he needed. Walton is a magnificent center, but they also know how to help him, with a great power forward in Lucas and backcourt speed."

If Portland team play did in fact make the real difference, it was still the incredible battle between Walton and Jabbar for which the series will be remembered. Former NBA referee and TV commentator Mendy Rudolph summed it up: "It was better to watch than the duels between Bill Russell and Wilt Chamberlain. More finesse."

Abdul-Jabbar outperformed Walton statistically—127–

The Pride of Portland

77 in points, 64-59 in rebounds—but as Curry Kirkpatrick reported in *Sports Illustrated*, "Walton seemed to control every key rebound, throw every smart pass and convert every big play his team needed." And it was Walton's team who advanced to the finals.

7

ROUND FOUR:
Portland Trail Blazers
vs.
Philadelphia 76ers

*T*HERE ARE FEW EVENTS that animate a city like having a team involved in a major sports championship. For a few precious days the hassles and problems of urban life recede far into the background, as talk of the championship dominates gatherings from school yards to corporate offices to bridge parties. It's the magic of a love affair and the thrills of a carnival all in one.

For Portland, the joy was even sweeter, because this was first love. Seldom has any city been privileged to have a team that so perfectly personified the virtues on which the city prided itself—togetherness, discipline, self-sacrifice, hard work. And seldom has a city responded to a team the way Portland did to the Blazers. Blazermania was a special kind of sport romance.

On May 17, four days after the Blazer's victory over LA, Portland's opponent was determined—the Philadelphia 76ers, who finally got by a stubborn Houston team in six games. Game One was set for May 22, in Philadelphia.

No team in the NBA was more different from Portland in every respect than the Philadelphia 76ers. On paper

The Pride of Portland

they were by far the best team in the league. But their awesome individual talent was often overshadowed by the clashes and controversies that swirled around the team like tornadoes.

The Philadelphia roster was:

No.	Player	Pos.	Ht.	Wt.	Yrs.	College
14	Henry Bibby	G	6' 1"	185	4	UCLA
23	Joe Bryant	F	6' 9"	210	1	LaSalle
42	Harvey Catchings	C	6' 9"	230	2	Hardin-Simmons
20	Doug Collins	G	6' 6"	180	4	Illinois State
53	Darryl Dawkins	C	6' 11"	252	1	Evans High School
10	Mike Donleavy	G	6' 3"	180	R	South Carolina
6	Julius Erving	F	6' 6"	200	5	Massachusetts
21	Lloyd Free	G	6' 1"	185	1	Guilford
25	Terry Furlow	F	6' 6"	190	R	Michigan State
11	Caldwell Jones	C	7' 1"	225	3	Albany State
30	George McGinnis	F	6' 8"	240	5	Indiana
50	Steve Mix	F	6' 7"	225	6	Toledo

The Portland Trail Blazers had been built from cellar dweller to champions by shrewd drafting and trading. The 76ers were put together with lots of cold hard cash. Philadelphia had plummeted to the very bottom of the NBA in 1972–73 (their 9–73 record was the worst in basketball history). They remained in the cellar for two more years, until owner Fitz Dixon enticed George McGinnis from Indiana of the ABA. In 1975–76 Philadelphia posted a 46–36 mark.

When Dixon snagged Julius Erving and Caldwell Jones for the next season, every NBA observer predicted a championship. But this collection of super athletes only managed to garner four more victories than the team of a year before. The problem was a clash of abilities and personalities.

The core of the team, and the core of many of the problems, were the $9-million forwards, George McGinnis and Julius Erving. The powerful McGinnis was a superior one-on-one player with a good (if unorthodox) outside shot (he made a surprising 62 three-point baskets his last season in the ABA). McGinnis had a superior season in 1976–77, averaged 21.4 points per game, 11.5 rebounds (eighth in the league), and boosted his shooting percentage from 41.7 to a very respectable 45.8. McGinnis, however, was not a particularly good passer and did not move well without the ball. He played a spotty, gambling sort of defense that far too frequently allowed his opponent to slip away for easy buckets. Although he was named team captain, he was not a leader. He hated to practice, and more than anyone was responsible for a clowning, rowdy atmosphere that made 76er practices disorganized shambles.

Julius Erving was very simply the most spectacular offensive player in basketball. His mind-boggling, acrobatic dunk shots made him the league's premier gate attraction (Philadelphia sold out 33 of its 41 road games). But despite averaging 21.6 points per game, Dr. J never felt comfortable. Although, contrary to some published reports, McGinnis welcomed rather than resented Erving's acquisition, neither the big power forward nor any other of the 76ers were willing to modify their games to accommodate the unique talents of the Doctor. As a result, Julius often went long periods without touching the ball; when he did get it, it was often too far away from the basket for him to properly execute his spectacular moves. On defense, Erving had quickness and intelligence to go along with great shot-blocking ability, but he too had a tendency to go for the steal to set up a crowd-pleasing dunk.

Erving couldn't get the ball enough, but the centers never saw it at all. Caldwell Jones, who had averaged nearly 20 points per game with San Diego of the ABA, averaged just five shots a game during the season, and most of those came off offensive rebounds. Jones was a premier shot blocker (fifth in the league), but a disappointing rebounder. Daryl Dawkins, at age 20, was an imposing physical specimen. He had come into the league directly from Evans High School in Orlando, Florida, and he had demonstrated the potential to become the most intimidating force in the league. But in his first two years, though occasionally spectacular, he was mostly unreliable. His play was seriously crippled by his inability to control his temper. He often screamed at the coach when taken out of a game. The third center, Harvey Catchings, was perhaps the quickest and best defensive player of the three. Catchings had started at the beginning of the year, but after an elbow separation he had seen little playing time. Like Jones, he was a fine shot blocker but mediocre rebounder.

Twenty-five-year-old Doug Collins was on the verge of becoming an All-Pro guard. A star in college and a starter on the 1972 Olympic team, Collins was a fine shooter and adequate ball handler. He moved without the ball better than any guard in the league, which gave him many high-percentage layups.

Jack Ramsay called Henry Bibby the most valuable player on the 76ers. A teammate of Walton's at UCLA, Bibby was an excellent playmaker, a tenacious defender, and he had a fine basketball intelligence. His job was to get the ball to the scorers, and he provided whatever organization there was in the Philadelphia offense.

Philadelphia's bench included reserves that could start for other teams around the league. Rugged veteran forward Steve Mix, who had been picked up by the 76ers after being out of basketball in the 1972–73 season, provided tenacious defense, steady rebounding, and high-percentage shooting (.523). Guard Lloyd Free was a great leaper and shooter who provided instant offense off the bench. Unfortunately, Free, self-designated "All-World," had an ego at least as large as his talent. He was given to showboating, often played negligible defense, and took too many bad shots.

Forward Joe Bryant was a talented shooter with excellent range. But he also had an ego problem, and loudly resented his limited playing time as fourth forward.

What little time was left after the first ten men got through divvying it up was shared by rookies Mike Dunleavy and Terry Furlow. Dunleavy, a sixth-round draft choice, hustled his way onto the roster over more talented players, and had hit for 32 points against the Blazers in a regular season game. Furlow was an excellent shooter and fine prospect.

The highest paid coach in the NBA ($200,000 per year), Gene Shue found himself more frequently playing traffic cop than coaching. A fine offensive guard for 11 years, Shue preferred a more disciplined, patterned style than the playground ball the Sixers fell into. For the playoffs, he hoped to keep the shouting and pouting down to a minimum.

Opinion was sharply divided around the league on who would win what Denver general manager Carl Sheer called "a classic match-up of team basketball versus overwhelming individual talent." Washington General Manager Bob Ferry summed up the arguments of Philly supporters. "Got to go with Philly with homecourt advantage and their depth. Portland forced LA to move the ball quickly by pressing. But running is Philly's game. You're really going to see what Bibby's made of. He's gonna control things. Know when to run, when to stop."

But John Havlicek, the key player on so many Celtic championship teams, liked Portland. "In the LA series Portland seemed to be so consistent in what they're doing. Based on that round you've got to make them the favorite, I think. Reason being they have all the necessary ingre-

The Pride of Portland

dients that go into a championship club. Big, good center in Walton. Great power forward in Lucas. Small, quick forward in Gross. Deep in the backcourt. Hollins is the best but others are ready to play any role. And they come off the bench with good strength, too. Every championship team I played on had those ingredients." Dave Debusschere, the stalwart of the Knicks' 1970 and 1973 NBA crowns, agreed with Havlicek. "Portland's got a bunch of unselfish players and remind me of the Knick and Celtic teams that went all the way."

Those who looked carefully at the four regular season games played between the two teams found little to indicate an advantage either way. Each team had won both their home games: Portland an early season 145–104 blowout and a 108–107 squeaker; Philadelphia a similar 108–107 game and a late season 128–116 win.

Jack Ramsay knew what his team would have to do to win. "We can't let them run and we can't let them set up their offense." Ramsay planned to curtail the Philly break by minimizing turnovers, hitting the offensive boards hard, and shutting off the outlet pass. If Philadelphia didn't break, the Blazers planned to clog the middle, keeping Erving and McGinnis away from the basket. Furthermore, a key strategy that worked so well against Los Angeles was to pressure the guards as they brought the ball up court, in an attempt to make the team set up its offense further away from the basket. A frustrated Philadelphia team, Ramsay knew, would soon start throwing up poor percentage bombs from far outside.

On offense, Ramsay planned to stick with his own aggressive attack. If the ball got into Walton, Erving and McGinnis were susceptible to back-door moves freeing Lucas and Gross. Ramsay felt his guards had a speed advantage over the Philadelphia guards, and he wanted to get his own fast break going as much as possible.

HIGHLIGHTS OF THE
BLAZERS' 1977 CHAMPIONSHIP SEASON

A WINNER. Fans mob Bill Walton after he and his teammates defeated the Philadelphia 76ers 109–107 to win the NBA 1977 crown in Portland. Walton scored 20 points and grabbed 23 rebounds. (This and all photos following courtesy World Wide Photos.)

TYPICAL TRAIL BLAZERS HARD DRIVING. Johnny Davis (16) comes down atop Chicago Bulls' Tate Armstrong (14) after making a shot during the first half in Chicago.

SIDELINED. In painfully restricted posture, Bill Walton sits on the bench in street clothes during game with Detroit Pistons. Walton had fallen on the ice in Chicago injuring his left knee.

FRUSTRATION. Boston's Sidney Wicks sprawls on the court after the ball was stolen from him by Portland's Bob Gross. Gross dunked the ball and the Blazers routed Boston 128–84. It was Wicks' first time in Portland since he was sold by the Blazers to the Celtics.

ROUGH PLAY. Maurice Lucas and Lionel Hollins rush for the ball while Indiana's Dave Robisch appears to take a hard one in the face.

DRIVE TIME. Portland's Dave Twardzik drives on Boston's Jo Jo White during the Trail Blazers' 104–99 victory over the Celtics. Twardzik raised his NBA leading field goal percentage to .707.

WATCHING HIS SHOT. Portland Trail Blazers' Bill Walton (32) keeps his eye on the ball as it goes in during game against Milwaukee. Also watching the shot is the Bucks' Brian Winters (32) Walton scored 32 points to lead the Trail Blazers to a 109–106 victory.

WINNERS. Fans show their support after their team captured the NBA title by defeating the Philadelphia 76ers 109-107 in Portland.

The Pride of Portland

It was the Portland speed that primarily bothered Gene Shue: "They have great quickness. There just isn't any team in the league like Portland. They gear their offense to their defense. They play fast break basketball. Their style has given us fits all year."

On offense, Shue was most worried about the pressure Portland would apply to his guards, who were not superior ball handlers. He closed his practice sessions—even to the ushers and ball boys—as he worked out a strategy to counter the Portland defense.

With the two teams so evenly matched, many observers felt the homecourt advantage that had played so prominent a role in the NBA that year could be the key factor. Jack Ramsay was asked by the Associated Press about Philadelphia's homecourt advantage: "After what we've been through," he said, "I honestly don't know how to read it. We beat both Denver and LA on their own courts and made it stick. But against Chicago we had the advantage and needed it." The odds makers read the homecourt advantage as critical. They established Philadelphia as 6–7 favorites to win the series, and five-point favorites for the first game.

Philadelphia remained the favorite right up to game time, despite some injuries that Portland felt increased their chances. Lloyd Free had suffered a bruised rib and partially collapsed lung in the Eastern Conference Final. He was not expected to play in the first game, meaning Bibby and Collins would have to keep pace with Portland's lightning-quick four-man guard crew for the whole game. George McGinnis' shooting slump was aggravated by a groin pull. Steve Mix had a bad ankle, and Darryl Dawkins was troubled by blurred vision.

But in the opening seconds of Game One, the capacity Spectrum crowd found out that injuries weren't a problem if you had a Doctor in the house. Caldwell Jones tipped the ball to Julius Erving, who sped solo down the court for a spectacular flying one-handed dunk. The Blazers, left standing on their heels at midcourt, seemed startled. This play was a perfect symbol of a game in which it was the 76ers who seemed more in control and better prepared, while the Blazers appeared tentative and, at times, disorganized.

The key element in Philadelphia's preparation was Gene Shue's secret plan to defuse Portland's defensive pressure. Seven-footer Caldwell Jones was bringing the ball up court by himself, while the Sixer guards moved far into the offensive zone. Shue explained his strategy after the game: "I have always believed in attacking a team's weaknesses. Portland's strength is its press, but the weakest guy in that tactic is Bill Walton. So we decided to switch to C.J."

The strategy worked perfectly. For a while, the Blazers tried to cover Jones, but the Sixers switched the duties to McGinnis. The Portland guards seemed totally confused and disoriented, and the strategy may have taken them out of the game. Neither Hollins nor Davis could generate any offense, they couldn't seem to get the ball up court, and at the other end of the floor, Collins went over and around Hollins at will.

Despite being badly outplayed at guard, Portland hung close on the brilliant play of Bill Walton and Maurice Lucas. There were 13 ties in the first half, and two Hollins free throws kept the Blazers within two at the half, 55–53.

Collins and Erving scored 25 of Philadelphia's 31 third-quarter points as the Sixers built an eight-point lead. Philadelphia penetration was getting Portland into serious foul trouble, as Gross and Steele alone picked up ten fouls trying to stop the elusive Dr. J. Lucas, weakened by a virus, and Hollins were also in serious trouble. Although the Blazers had a slight advantage from the floor, the Sixers

The Pride of Portland

converted 24 straight free throws in the middle of the game to keep themselves on top.

The Blazers, led by Walton, outscored Philadelphia 9–2 in the first 3:12 of the fourth period to narrow the gap to one, 88–87. Erving scored twice as Philly moved ahead once again. With 2:46 left, Lucas went on a mini-spurt, hitting two 20-foot jumpers and finding Walton with a brilliant pass that narrowed the lead to two, 101–99.

Unfortunately, at that point, fouls once again told the tale. Lucas picked up a "phantom" foul, his sixth, with 1:29 left. Giant Darryl Dawkins promptly sunk two charity tosses, added another a few seconds later, then stole the ball from Steele and found Doug Collins for the ice-breaking basket. The Sixers won the important first game, 107–101.

This game was one in which the usually important shooting and rebounding statistics didn't tell the story. The Blazers outshot the Sixers .511 to .435, and outrebounded them 48–38. However, Portland committed an astounding 34 turnovers which led to 26 Philadelphia points. The normally error-prone 76ers only committed 20 turnovers, which led to 11 points. Despite the rebounding edge, Philadelphia shut off the outlet pass so effectively the Blazers only scored four fast break baskets for the entire game. Without Walton's 28 points and 20 rebounds, Lucas' 18 points, and Gross's eight for ten shooting for 16, the Blazers would have been far out of the game.

For the Sixers, George McGinnis continued his shooting slump, hitting only three of 12 shots in 22 minutes. But Julius Erving, with 33, and Doug Collins, with 30, more than made up for his problems. Henry Bibby played great defense and a terrific floor game. Big center Caldwell Jones had eight points and 11 rebounds to go along with his excellent ball handling.

After looking at the game film, Jack Ramsay analyzed

the game for the AP: "It's hard to win a game when you make 34 turnovers—our average is about 17. We gave them fast break opportunities. We didn't run our offense effectively. We didn't pass the ball crisply, we didn't come to meet the ball with authority. We didn't have steals from our guards in the backcourt. But the fact that we can play as ineffectively as we did and still be in the game at the end should show something."

Ramsay admitted he was surprised by the Sixer tactic of the center bringing up the ball. But he didn't think the ploy would have a lasting effect on the series: "The fact that they bring up the ball with somebody other than their guards really doesn't affect how we're going to play defense. Our defense is predicated on stopping their running game and making them play half-court offense. If they're going to bring up the ball with a big player, that's not a factor because it means they have to start their offense even higher."

Some observers suggested that Portland's nine-day layoff between the LA and Philadelphia series had made his team rusty. But Ramsay dismissed that. "I think we were overanxious," he said flatly, "not stale."

If the Blazers were overanxious in Game One, they were completely outplayed in Game Two, held in the Spectrum on Thursday, May 26. The Philadelphia strategy was obvious as they collapsed even tighter on Walton and Lucas, again forcing the Portland guards, who had such a poor game on Sunday, to shoot from the perimeter.

Portland hung close for most of the first period, before Philadelphia scored the last five points of the quarter to take a 31–25 lead. Then the Sixers came back on the court to blow the Blazers off the court in a stunning display of fast break basketball.

The Blazers could do absolutely nothing right. They shot 22 percent for the quarter and committed seven turn-

The Pride of Portland

overs (to go along with the nine they had in the first period). Walton didn't score a point, as the guards were completely unable to get him the ball. Philadelphia, on the other hand, scored eight layups in the period en route to 59 percent shooting and a 61–43.

Philadelphia maintained its advantage with ease in the second half as the four Portland guards—Hollins, Twardzik, Davis, and Gilliam—could not generate any offense. The 76ers, getting looser and more brazenly confident as the game wore on, became more physical. Players on the court could feel tension building. With 4:29 left in the game and the Sixers up 96–76, the volcano erupted, producing the ugliest incident of the year.

The trouble began when massive Darryl Dawkins went over the back of Bobby Gross as a Herm Gilliam shot caromed off the rim. Angered by Gross's refusal to let go of the ball, Dawkins hurled the much smaller Gross to the floor. Gross popped up, enraged, and confronted the 20-year-old center. After a moment of tension, Dawkins unleashed a roundhouse right that missed Gross and hit his teammate Doug Collins, who was trying to pull Gross away. Collins later needed four stitches.

Fans and players spilled onto the court, led by Ramsay and the Blazers' enforcer, Maurice Lucas. Lucas raced to Dawkins and stunned him with a right to the head. They squared off for combat, but fortunately were separated before any further blows could be struck. It took police and security guards more than ten minutes to clear the floor. Lucas and Dawkins were ejected from the game.

Dawkins wasn't through, however. Still blind with anger, mostly directed at his teammates, whom he felt didn't give him adequate support, he roared into the locker room and destroyed a commode, a dozen chairs, a couple of wall lockers, and a metal partition.

Back on the floor, the game ended with Portland going

down to defeat, 107–89. In by far their worst game of the playoffs, the Blazers shot only .356 to Philly's .482. The supposedly one-on-one Sixers outassisted Portland 33–21, a statistic which demonstrated how completely the Portland offense had broken down. The collapsing Philadelphia defense took Walton out of the game, and he was outscored by the Philadelphia centers 18–17, and outrebounded 19–16. Lucas was seven for 19 from the floor, Gross four for ten, Hollins six for 18, Davis three for eight, and Gilliam zero for four.

Philadelphia was once again led by Collins with 27 and Dr. J with 20. Henry Bibby added 15 points and a terrific 11 assists. In the locker room, George McGinnis described the key to Philly's success: "We scored lay-in after lay-in after lay-in. I guarantee you we got triple what they got off the break. Even more. Every time I turned around someone was scoring an easy one."

In the Blazer locker room, Herm Gilliam described what he felt was his team's problem: "We play great as a team but we're almost playing exclusively one-on-one now. We don't win that way. They're the ones with the individual moves. But it seems we're playing their game, not ours." Said Maurice Lucas, "We're hurrying the game to a certain extent. We're shooting the ball before we've even had it. We've got to penetrate more." Jack Ramsay summed it all up: "They're beating us because of our ineffective offense. Our guards initiate our offense and when we're playing team ball everyone benefits. When the shot goes up without the ball ever getting back to our guards, it shows we're all not involved."

The Blazers had two assets as they regrouped from the two defeats in Philadelphia. One was their superb basketball intelligence, combined with the endless drilling and discipline Ramsay had enforced all season. The Portland players still had confidence in themselves and in their

The Pride of Portland

coach, and they knew that could and would get them back to executing their game plan.

The second asset, their best tonic all season, was the return to the friendly confines of Memorial Coliseum and their legion of Blazer fans. Several times, especially early in the season, the Blazers had limped in off a tough road trip only to find new life before the enthusiasm of the home crowd.

In the return home, though, there was one worry that was expressed by the NBA office—that the Portland fans might respond in kind to the incident in Philadelphia and the resulting bad behavior by a tiny portion of the Spectrum crowd.

Commissioner Larry O'Brian was determined not to let the series get out of hand. He fined Lucas and Dawkins $2,500 apiece, and sent them the following stern telegram: "Your conduct could have resulted in a serious injury to another player and it created the potential for a violent crowd reaction that might have led to serious injury to innocent spectators. The type of conduct you displayed will not be tolerated. You are hereby informed that any similar action on your part during the remainder of the series will be dealt with even more severely."

In telegrams to Gene Shue and Jack Ramsay, the commissioner warned, "I expect each of you to exert leadership and to meet your responsibilities during the remainder of the series to make certain there is no repetition of such an incident."

O'Brian needn't have worried about either the Portland crowd or team. A public address announcement before the game appealed for sportsmanship, and the crowd of 12,923 immediately responded with wholesome enthusiasm. As Maurice Lucas was being introduced, he ran over to the Philadelphia bench and shook hands with the surprised Dawkins. This sportsmanlike conduct further quieted the fans. But, again demonstrating his keen intelligence, Lucas later explained his gesture wasn't quite 100 percent noble: "It was that old Marquette con. You think I didn't learn anything from Al [McGuire]?"

For whatever combination of reasons—Portland's intelligence, coaching, homecourt advantage—an entirely new playoff series began with the opening tip at 12:30 P.M. on Sunday, May 29. After an opening basket by Doug Collins, the Blazers finally began to play like the team that had smashed Los Angeles. The fast break returned in full glory as Portland raced to a 32–12 lead in the first ten minutes. The long-lost guards were reintegrated into the offense, and Johnny Davis sprinted for ten points during the first-quarter spurt. When the buzzer sounded with the score Portland 34, Philadelphia 21, the Blazers had attained, for the first time in the series, the first-quarter advantage that had been the trademark of their regular season success.

Led once more by Collins and Erving, and aided considerably by free throws, Philadelphia came back with a 32-point second quarter to cut the halftime margin to seven. But the Blazers continued to play loose, confident basketball, rebounding with authority, moving without the ball, attacking aggressively on defense. Gradually, as the game moved into the fourth quarter, the strain of keeping up with the running Blazers began to tell on the key Philadelphia players.

With Lloyd Free available only for very limited duty, Bibby and Collins had played, respectively, 85 and 80 minutes in the first two games. In Game Three, they grew weary chasing the four Portland guards. Julius Erving had played 82 minutes in the first two games; there was no substitute on the Philadelphia bench, or for that matter, in the NBA, who could come in and take over for the incredible Dr. J. In this game, Julius was done in by the double strain of providing the bulk of his team's offense, as well as

The Pride of Portland

chasing Bobby Gross, who scored 19 points. With two and a half minutes gone in the fourth, Walton hit two spectacular shots—a tip-in and a stuff after a steal—to trigger a 26–10 spurt that upped the lead from four points to 20. The Blazers coasted home with their first win, 129–107.

Portland's outstanding team game relieved the pressure on Bill Walton, who responded with 20 points, 18 rebounds, and nine assists. Lucas added 27 points, 12 rebounds, and five assists. For the first time, the backcourt figured prominently in the scoring, as Davis hit 18 and Hollins, though still in a shooting slump from the floor, converted seven of nine from the line for 15 points. Off the bench, Lloyd Neal added 13 points in just 17 minutes.

More important than the individual statistics were the team figures. Portland outshot Philadelphia 49 percent to 46 percent, and for the third straight game outrebounded them, 52–44. They doubled the Philly total with 34 assists. Perhaps most significantly, they had only 16 turnovers (after 34 and 29 in Games One and Two), and they upped their steals to 13 (after eight and nine in the first two games).

Julius Erving led Philadelphia with 28 points, and Collins hit nine of 13 from the floor on the way to 21 points. The only other Sixer in double figures was George McGinnis, who managed 14 points despite six of 17 shooting.

In the Portland locker room after the game, the jubilant squad knew they'd corrected their mistakes of the first two games. Bill Walton said, "I think we were ahead the whole game. I think that's important. In the first two we played catch-up ball and were overanxious to put points on the board. I think it's important that everyone handle the ball. Shooting should only result when the opportunity presents itself. If you don't handle the ball, you lose your feel for it. Then when you do get it, you don't necessarily play well."

In the Philadelphia locker room, Gene Shue commented, "They were much more aggressive and much quicker than in the first two games." But he added, "I wasn't particularly disappointed in the way we played, and I didn't think our team was flat. They're just very tough to beat on their own court and they got off to a good lead, which is something I didn't want to happen."

Shue might not have been disappointed in his team's play, but he had to be worried about the bickering that was beginning to erupt on his team. Though pronounced 85 percent fit by team physicians, Lloyd Free complained constantly about his bruised rib and demanded to be sent home. Forward Joe Bryant lashed out at Steve Mix, accusing him of not giving 100 percent and saying he, Bryant, should be playing instead. Instead of providing encouragement and moral support to the slumping McGinnis, his teammates laughed at him in practice, and shouted "Brick" (NBA slang for a horrible shot) every time the big forward released the ball.

Game Four was played on May 31 in Memorial Coliseum, and Philadelphia seemed to leave both their game plan and their composure in the locker room. After a 2-2 tie, the Blazers, led by Hollins, Lucas, and Walton, roared to a 19-4 advantage. The Blazers hit nine of their first ten shots, while Philadelphia shot a measly 22 percent. The Sixers hurried, and went completely away from their inside game. Seven first-quarter turnovers led to nine Portland points.

The Blazers got a little lackadaisical in the second quarter, as Julius Erving, who had 18 points, brought Philly back to within 11 at the half, 57-46. Collins cut the lead to seven in the opening minute of the second half, but Lionel Hollins, finally breaking out of his shooting slump, took over. He connected for a three-point play, then after a McGinnis bucket, took a Lucas pass and hit from the top of

The Pride of Portland

the key. After a Walton block on Dr. J, Lionel took a feed from Davis and stuffed the ball. He completed his run by finding Walton with a pinpoint pass for another dunk. The lead was back to 14.

Despite the Portland advantage, however, the Portland fans were stunned as Walton picked up his fifth personal foul with 7:02 left in the third quarter. Fourteen points looked very small as Lloyd Neal came in to join Lucas, Hollins, Davis, and Calhoun.

But the Blazermaniacs' worries were swept away as the Blazer subs, in a breathtaking display of team basketball, proceeded to outscore Philadelphia 27-10 for a 98-67 advantage at the end of three. From that point, the lead stretched out, once reaching 41 points; the final margin was an awesome 130-98. The 32-point spread was the third largest in NBA playoff history (the '61 Celtics defeated St. Louis by 34; the '65 Celtics bested LA by 33 and 32 points).

After the game, the Philadelphia team was subdued. "They truly embarrassed us," Doug Collins said. "They ran all over us in front of millions of people." The "embarrassment" included Portland's outshooting Philadelphia 56 percent to 44 percent, scoring 21 more field goals, and forcing 30 Sixer turnovers that led to 40 Blazer points.

One of the best benefits of the game was that it gave the Portland starters some badly needed rest. Bill Walton played only 26 minutes, yet he scored 12 points, grabbed 13 rebounds, and dished out seven assists. Maurice Lucas scored 24 points and snared 12 rebounds in 28 minutes. Lionel Hollins broke out of his shooting slump to hit for 25 points in his 33 minutes of playing time.

George McGinnis commented on Portland's play: "Portland plays blackboard basketball. They really move the ball. No messing around. Everyone seems to be in position for a layup or a 10-foot jump shot. When they're on they really make you look bad. No doubt about it. We had three guys hustling back on defense several times and they had four guys hustling back on offense. We work our butts off to get Walton in foul trouble and what happens? They play twice as good as before. They crushed our offense and ripped open our defense."

Portland's landslide victory had tied the series at two games apiece. The Blazers had little time to bask in the glow of their rout, as they had to head back to Philadelphia for Game Five. Said Jack Ramsay, "The margin of victory [in Game Four] doesn't mean anything. We played an excellent game, and we won, but all it means is that we now enter a two-of-three series with two of the games on their court. We now have to show we can take the kind of game we played here twice and produce it there. We didn't do it the first two games, we've got our work cut out for us."

There was no question that Game Five, scheduled for 9:00 P.M. on Friday, June 3, was the key game for the Blazers. They had to win a game in the Spectrum to win the championship, and they didn't want to have to do it in a seventh game. The pressure was also on Philadelphia—they had to rebound from the two drubbings in Oregon and maintain their homecourt advantage.

With so much at stake, both teams were tight in the first half of Game Five. Portland was only able to manage 38 percent shooting, but the 76ers shot an even worse 29 percent. The Blazers went in front 22–15 at the end of one, reached an 11-point advantage at 34–23, then watched Dr. J once again bring Philadelphia back. The halftime score was Portland 45, Philadelphia 41. Erving had 20 points, nearly half Philly's total.

The 76ers closed within one, 53–52, in the first four minutes of the third quarter. George McGinnis missed a free throw that could have tied the game at 53, then Dr. J failed to connect on a jumper that could have given Philadelphia their first lead. Perhaps inspired by the two failures of the two Philadelphia superstars, the Blazers suddenly ignited. In an awesome display of classic fast break basketball, the Blazers outscored the 76ers 17-2 for the next five minutes, 32-14 for the rest of the quarter. As the dust settled at the end of the Blazers' third 40-point quarter in three games, they had a nineteen-point advantage, 85-66.

Hero of the charge was small forward Bobby Gross. Bob raced up and down the court for 11 third-quarter points, while holding the red-hot Dr. J to just four. Walton's defense and rebounding triggered the blistering break, and Hollins and Twardzik ran circles around the tired Philly guards.

However, Philadelphia was not about to lay down and die in front of their home crowd. Portland had increased its lead to 91-69 with 8:28 left. Then Julius Erving got back on track, and Joe Bryant came off the bench to toss in seven. But Lucas, Twardzik, Hollins, Calhoun, and Walton held them off as the Blazers took the game they had to win, 110-104.

Once again the statistics reflected Portland's superb team plan. Bob Gross led the team with 25 points in just 25 minutes. Lucas had 20 points and 13 rebounds. Walton only had 14 points, but he had a career playoff high 24 boards. Hollins, Davis, and Twardzik combined for 41 points. As a team, Portland outshot the 76ers .453 to .391 and outrebounded them 59-47.

Once again, the Philadelphia story was Julius Erving, who had 37 points and seven assists. Despite his magnificent performance, Dr. J was tormented by his team's collapse in the third quarter. He commented, "Everything that possibly could go wrong went wrong. It was the strangest quarter I ever saw. I can't put my finger on all of them, but so many things that were supposed to be there just weren't there. So many parts were missing. Our defense just fell apart. All season long we're the team with the fast break. We know about the break and we should know how to stop them. We just couldn't."

In the Portland locker room, a happy Jack Ramsay said, "Everything we're doing is a team effort. Everyone is just doing his job. Our defense gave us the fast break. It also gave us the bulge against their fourth-quarter comeback. We were shaken by them, but we never lost our poise."

If the Blazers remained cool, the Beaver State's 2 million citizens were going out of their minds with joy. Five hundred fans greeted the Blazer plane at 4:30 A.M. Scalpers were asking and getting outrageous prices for the precious tickets to the game which, Blazermaniacs were convinced, would end with the Blazers being crowned NBA kings.

But the Portland coaches and team were far from overconfident. Only one previous team in NBA history had come back from a 2–0 deficit to win the championship (the '69 Celtics), while 13 had failed. Only the 1949 Minneapolis Lakers had won the title in their first playoff appearance. The confusion and constant bickering to which Phildelphia had fallen victim tended to make people forget they were a team of superbly talented athletes who could explode at any time.

On Sunday, June 5, a record crowd of 12,951 frenzied fans saw the NBA's two best teams play a magnificent basketball game. George McGinnis hit three fast shots for Philadelphia as they forged an eight-point lead midway through the first quarter. With his shooting touch magically restored, the muscular forward's confidence and aggressiveness returned, and he played Maurice Lucas more than even throughout the game.

At the eight-minute mark of the first quarter, Portland

The Pride of Portland

got a key break. Caldwell Jones picked up his third foul and went to the bench. Darryl Dawkins replaced him and Lloyd Free came in for Collins, but that turned out to be a bad combination for Philadelphia. Led by Bill Walton, who had 13 points, 12 rebounds, four assists, and four blocked shots in the half, the Blazers outscored the 76ers 39–20 in the next 13 minutes en route to a 67–55 halftime lead. For the fourth time in four games, Portland had a 40-point quarter. That sign, along with the 12-point lead and the homecourt advantage, led many Blazer supporters to think the game was in the bag.

The game might well have been, if it hadn't been for the heroics of Julius Erving. The reemergence of his front court partner McGinnis gave the Doctor more operating room, and despite the frantic efforts of Bob Gross, who was himself having a fine offensive game, Julius was unstoppable. He soared over and around the Portland defense for a series-high 40 points that prevented the Blazers from pulling away.

Portland maintained its 12-point lead until late in the fourth quarter. Philadelphia cut it to four with 4:40 left, but Lucas got the lead back to eight, 108–100, with 2:20 to go.

To Blazer fans, the final two minutes seemed like two years. Lloyd Free hit a free throw, then Dr. J hit a 20-foot jumper after a Blazer turnover. Walton was called for an offensive foul, and Erving hit two free throws. The lead was down to three.

Maurice Lucas went to the foul line for two vital free throws with 1:09 left. But only one went down, and the lead was four. Walton blocked a Philly shot, but McGinnis got the ball and popped in a jumper. The score was 109–107 with 18 seconds left.

Those 18 torturous seconds saw the most frenzied action of the entire playoffs. Both teams were exhausted. With the championship on the line, Portland had gone with its starters for almost all of the game—no starter played under 39 minutes. For the Sixers, Erving played 43 minutes, McGinnis 41, Collins 39.

It was Portland that first gave in to the pressure. George McGinnis tied up Bobby Gross without fouling. Big George won the resulting jump. Philadelphia had possession, needing just a basket to send the game into overtime.

Every basketball fan in the country knew who would get the ball—Julius Erving. The Doctor took the ball at the top of the key and went up with a 20-foot jumper. But this last try by the Sixers' gallant warrior failed.

The game still wasn't over, however. Six-foot Lloyd Free, a sensational leaper, snared the offensive rebound. He went up for a five-foot jumper from the baseline, but Gross and Hollins smothered him. Fortunately, a foul was not called. The Sixers had the ball out of bounds with three seconds left. The ball was inbounded to McGinnis, who whirled into the middle of the key and launched a 15-footer. It was short and fell off to the right, where Bill Walton was waiting. The giant redhead swatted the ball to midcourt, where Hollins grabbed it as the buzzer went off. The Portland Trail Blazers were the champions of professional basketball at last.

Memorial Coliseum turned into bedlam the instant the game ended. Bill Walton tore off his jersey and hurled it high in the air. A sea of Blazermaniacs swarmed onto the floor as the biggest mass party in Oregon history began.

Walton, as usual, led the Blazers in the last triumphant game. The Blazer center had 20 points, 23 rebounds, seven assists, and eight big blocked shots. Bob Gross continued his brilliant shooting of Game Five by hitting 12 of 16 for 24 points. Lucas, although held to three of 12 from the

The Pride of Portland

floor by the rejuvenated McGinnis, had ten rebounds and five assists.

The key to the victory, however, may have been the play of the guards. Davis, Hollins, and Twardzik outscored the Philadelphia guards 40–21. The return of McGinnis to the offense seemed to take Doug Collins out, and the 6'6" guard, who had played such a large role in the first five games, only got off nine shots, hitting a meager three for a total of six points.

Erving hit 17 of 29 from the floor and six of seven at the line for his 40 points. McGinnis added 28, but no other Sixer could manage more than ten. After the game, a gracious Julius Erving commented on the Blazers' victory: "They helped each other better than we did," he said. "They had cohesiveness. They had a consistent attitude toward the game that enabled them to win. It's all a matter of mental conditioning. They worked hard all year. They started with a basic game plan, it worked for them all season, and they stayed with it."

Cohesiveness, consistency, mental conditioning, hard work. Those had been the hallmarks of the Blazer team right from the first of their 109 games that led to the title. Nothing is more satisfying in life than setting a difficult goal, then working hard and persistently to accomplish it. For every single member of the Blazer organization this championship was the high point of their professional lives. Jack Ramsay, accepting the Poduloff Championship Trophy, said, "This is the finest team and the finest people I've ever coached. This is what I've aimed for since becoming a professional coach—but I would feel the same way and say the same thing about these people even if we hadn't won."

Just as Walton had been the heart of the team all season, he was the heart of the joyous postgame celebrations. The

The Pride of Portland

day after the game, 50,000 people lined the streets of Portland for a victory parade. Walton, dressed in cutoffs and a sweatshirt, his face marked by a big lipstick smear, romped like a kid, at one point gleefully dumping beer on the head of Mayor Neil Goldschmidt. In a ceremony at Federal Plaza, Walton told the crowd: "This is as much fun as I've ever had in any sport since I started playing when I was eight years old. I can't imagine it getting any better, but I'm sure you folks will find a way to make it that way."

TWO

PROFILES OF THE CHAMPIONS

8

JACK RAMSAY

"THIS TEAM WAS waiting for Jack Ramsay, and Jack Ramsay was waiting for this team. It's been a great marriage." *(Stu Inman)*

A photograph taken on June 5, 1977, captures the essence of why people choose—despite the agonies, frustrations, and tedium—to become professional sports coaches. The picture was of Dr. Jack Ramsay, the Portland Trail Blazers' "Bald-headed Emperor," arms thrown up and out over his head, which was tilted back to receive a deluge of sweet, cold champagne. His face, covered with wine, was formed into a smile that is a combination of bliss, relief, and triumph. The expression was simple, uncomplicated, and extraordinarily beautiful. That's what coaching is all about. "Nothing," said Ramsay, "in my professional life can top this. Nothing. We kept our team concept and we won it."

Team concept, team basketball won the championship for the Trail Blazers, and it was Ramsay, more than anyone else, who instilled in the Portland players the pride that led to victory. When the Blazers hired Jack Ramsay in the spring of 1976, they hired the best coach in professional basketball.

Ramsay's stature in the game was confirmed in a poll conducted by *Sport* magazine. A distinguished group of basketball professionals rated each coach in five areas: game coaching, game preparation, technical knowledge, handling players, and judging talent. Ramsay won in a landslide. His six-point margin over second-place finisher John MacLeod of the Phoenix Suns was larger than the points that separated the next seven coaches. Joe Axelson, general manager of the Kansas City Kings, summed up the panel's opinion of Ramsay: "In the course of a game, Ramsay sees and analyzes and rectifies more situations in one quarter than some coaches do in four. Ramsay responds quickly and decisively. His teams are in superb condition. His players are confident and disciplined. He uses time-outs to stop the other teams' momentum, or when his team's momentum is faltering. Also, he substitutes not for the sake of change but with a specific purpose in mind—such as capitalizing on mismatches or a particular player's weakness."

Many observers believe that Ramsay achieved so much success because he was one of those rare individuals whose philosophy of basketball matched his philosophy of life. Hard work, a commitment to honesty and cooperation, and devotion to physical fitness were Ramsay's personal characteristics long before he came to the City of Roses. Blazer trainer Ron Culp said, "It's one thing for a coach to say something like 'We must be physically fit.' It's another thing for him to really mean *we*. Jack really meant it." Another man who was convinced was Bill Walton: "Ramsay's the greatest. It's sure good to have a coach who puts out as much as he expects his players to put out."

Ramsay had been "putting out" since he started to play

basketball in a grade school league in Milford, Connecticut. As Ramsay explained in his excellent book *The Coach's Art*, even at that time he had begun to think analytically about the game of basketball: "The coach ... grouped his players around him. He turned to the biggest guy on the team. 'Batchelor,' he said, 'you're the rebounder. Every time you get a rebound or take the ball I want you to throw the ball to the other end of the floor.' Turning to me, he continued, 'Ramsay, I want you to be there to catch the ball, drive to the basket and shoot.' I rather liked that offense, and we had some early success with it. But before long the opposing team would keep a man with me as I raced for the open basket. Batchelor was soon throwing more interceptions than completions. That's when I began to think about defense winning ball games."

When he was a sophomore in high school Ramsay's family moved to Philadelphia. Ramsay played on three Pennsylvania state championship teams at Upper Darby High School. The Upper Darby coach, Bill Anderson, was a man who believed in organization and discipline, and those beliefs were firmly stamped on the young Ramsay.

A tryout during his senior year got Ramsay an athletic scholarship to St. Joseph's College in Philadelphia. After one year, the war interrupted Ramsay's collegiate career. But this interruption may have been a blessing, for in the Navy Ramsay had the chance to play against a wide variety of excellent competition. He returned to St. Joseph's a very much matured sophomore, and he became the team captain on a moderately successful collegiate squad. By the time he graduated in 1949, Ramsay had determined that he wanted one thing—a career in basketball.

His career aspirations required considerable sacrifices for himself and his family. High school coaching was not a lucrative profession, and Ramsay had to teach as well as coach. To learn more about the game Ramsay played in the Eastern Professional Basketball League and for another semi-pro team. To ensure his teaching success, he at the same time was taking the graduate courses that would eventually lead to his being awarded a doctorate. Looking at his schedule, one has to remark that a man who would conquer the exhaustion he must have faced would have to be successful in the future.

Ramsay's major career break came in 1956, at age thirty-one, when he was offered the head coaching job at his alma mater, St. Joseph's College. Taking the job meant a $3,000 pay cut, but Ramsay's commitment to his career was total. His decision turned out to be very fortunate.

In his very first season at the small school, Ramsay took a squad that had been 12–14 the year before and turned them into a 23–6 team that went on to postseason play. In 11 years at St. Joseph's, Ramsay led the Hawks to a 234–72 record; his worst season was 18–10; his teams participated in ten major postseason tournaments. By this time, Ramsay had developed his distinctive coaching style which was designed to get the maximum out of every ballplayer. Jack Finches, in *Signature* magazine, described Ramsay's St. Joseph squads: "A tireless, alert and mentally disciplined bunch of ball hawks with a minimal amount of top drawer talent."

After 11 years of college coaching, Ramsay began to have eye problems that may have been caused by stress. Irv Kosloff, owner of the Philadelphia 76ers, asked Ramsay to become that team's general manager, and he agreed. The 76ers, who had the incredible Wilt Chamberlain at center, as well as such superb performers as Chet Walker, Luke Jackson, Hal Greer, Larry Costello, and Billy Cunningham, compiled a 68–13 record and breezed through the playoffs on the way to the NBA crown. Ramsay later compared this 76er team to the champion Blazers: "That team [the 76ers] was certainly physically stronger than this one, and more apt to win decisively. And in those days there were teams in the league you knew you wouldn't lose to. However, this team is the best passing team. Every one of our players is a good passer, and when you have players who can and will pass, it makes for very good movement away from the ball."

After the 76ers championship season, a complicated series of problems involving Wilt Chamberlain brought Ramsay back to the coaching ranks as pilot of the 76ers. Chamberlain, after flirting with the idea of being a player coach with Ramsay as an assistant, decided he wanted to be traded and went off to the Lakers. Without a dominating center, Ramsay led the 76ers for four seasons and compiled a rcord of 174–154. The inability of the management of the Philadelphia franchise to correct the team's decline led him to then move on to coach the expansion Buffalo franchise.

It was at Buffalo that Ramsay's true genius as a professional coach began to emerge. After suffering through a season with a 21–61 record, Ramsay took Buffalo to an incredible three playoffs in a row. Over the next three seasons, this doormat franchise had the overall fourth best record in the NBA.

But after four seasons, Ramsay had a falling out with owner Paul Snyder. Ramsay's total commitment to teamwork and physical fitness didn't sit well with players like Bob McAdoo and Ernie DiGregorio. They thought Ramsay was a "nut," a goody-goody who was only interested in preventing them from having a good time. Snyder backed his high-priced stars and Ramsay resigned. The Portland Trail Blazers couldn't have been happier. Harry Glickman and Stu Inman had admired Ramsay's style for years, and in several meetings the management team discovered that their attitudes and Ramsay's jibed perfectly. The marriage of Ramsay and the Trail Blazers was one made in heaven.

The "Ramsay System" that led to the NBA Championship had several key elements. One was the commitment to physical conditioning. The grind of the 82-game NBA schedule is perhaps the most arduous in all of professional sports. A team whose members can avoid injury and who can play at nearly full energy for the entire game night after night will be winning teams. Jack Ramsay has always cared about fitness. He himself engaged in a whole range of vigorous activities ranging from surfing to jogging, tennis, swimming, bicycling, and jumping rope. His diet was based on sound nutritional principles. At age 52, he still had a 32-inch waist.

Ramsay instructed every Portland player to undergo a strenuous off-season conditioning program. Each player was required to be able to run a mile in under six minutes and to do 300 rope jumps in under two minutes. In addition, while at Buffalo, Ramsay had supervised the development of a series of stretching exercises with which his team began every practice. These exercises, which are designed to forestall muscle pulls and tears, have been adopted by other NBA teams.

A conditioned team, Ramsay believed, must next be a disciplined team. And discipline begins with proper organization of practices. Harry Glickman called Ramsay's practices "mini-clinics." Ramsay has said, "Players need organization and they want organization. I often post a copy of the practice schedule in the locker room so the players can see what they're trying to accomplish and why."

Getting his players to understand exactly why they were doing what they were doing was probably the key to Ramsay's extraordinary ability to communicate with his players. Basketball writer Charley Rosen has commented that "Portland wins because each player *embraces* his role and *trusts* that his teammates will accept and perform theirs." Players embraced Ramsay's team concept because, as Walton has said, "He makes you realize your limitations, and not only work within them, but extend them." Stu Inman summed it up: "Jack Ramsay has gotten the maximum efficiency from this team."

But getting each player to perform with maximum efficiency is not the entire job of a coach. For a team to play with maximum efficiency, the coach must be able to react to game situations, to sense the tempo and rhythm of a game, to react to what the other coach is doing. And at this side of the coach's task, Jack Ramsay has proved as skilled as he is in other areas.

A perfect example was a game in which Portland was trailing Chicago by two points with eight seconds left. Ramsay called a time-out and ordered a particular full-court press. He substituted a center for guard Johnny Davis so that the man inbounding the ball would be distracted. He substituted a quick guard, Larry Steele, for Maurice Lucas. Then Ramsay diagrammed Chicago's most frequently used out-of-bounds play and explained each Portland player's individual assignment. When the team returned to the court, the Chicago players cut, spun, set screens, but the Portland players made all the right moves in response. As time ticked away, the passer hurried his throw-in, Lionel Hollins stole the ball and scored. Again Chicago called time-out, and again Ramsay diagrammed a defense. Again Hollins stole the ball and scored the winning basket. When superbly conditioned, superbly prepared, superbly motivated players are directed by a superbly talented man like Ramsay, fans witness the finest example of the coach's art. Ramsay's art brought Portland an NBA crown in 1977.

9

BILL WALTON

"**W**ALTON'S SUCH A COMPLETE PLAYER, with no weaknesses; he could play in this league if he were only six feet tall." (*Red Holzman, Coach, New York Knicks*)

"He's strange." (*Anonymous newsman*)

Perhaps no athlete in the past decade has aroused a wider range of fan emotions or experienced a more turbulent career than Bill Walton. At times labeled a "malingerer," a "freak," a "communist," at other times the object of universal affection, Walton has remained an enigma, as unpredictable off the court as he is consistent on. But there is no doubt that every Portland fan will go to his grave thanking providence for bringing Walton to the Blazers for the 1976-77 season.

On court, Walton's brilliance was unquestioned. "Bill Walton," said Jack Ramsay, "is more skilled in all facets of the game than any of the dominant centers in NBA history. Wilt was a great rebounder and shot blocker and scorer but he had no range and he was a terrible foul shooter. Bill

The Pride of Portland

Russell was the best defensively, a fierce competitor. Kareem is the best offensive player of the three. But to me, Bill does all of those things well. Bill is a great, great center." John Wooden has often been quoted as saying that "William was the most unselfish player I ever coached." Extremely high praise from a man whose UCLA players epitomized team basketball and who is not given by disposition to accolades of any kind.

Tom Meschery, a Blazer assistant coach in Walton's first two years in the NBA, has said that Walton "was no ordinary ballplayer. He studied the game. If the average pro basketball player could be compared to someone who holds a master's degree, Bill Walton has a Ph.D."

Al Attles, coach of the Golden State Warriors, addressed Walton's team skills from a different angle when answering the question: "What's the first thing that comes to your mind when you think of Bill Walton as a basketball player?" "He'd be fun to play with. The kind of player you might get the ball back from if you pass it to him." "Bill's greatest assets," said Maurice Lucas, "are passing and rebounding. Those are mine too. And I would have to say that movement and passing are the biggest reasons Portland has been so successful the past two seasons." Walton obviously agreed: "Offensive basketball should be five players *constantly moving* with the basic intent of getting the ball to the person *closest to the basket*." If one thought all those self-effacing thoughts were a little too good to be true, that hint of cynicism faded when the Portland Trail Blazers played their game in the 1976–77 season.

First the ball was pushed up court providing more time, should the fast break opportunity not be there, to run plays through completely, to keep the defense concentrating for 17 or 18 seconds rather than ten or 12 seconds. Then regularly, the ball zipped into Walton at either the low or high post. Then a weak side pick would free Lucas for a quickly launched jumper; or Gross would fake out, then zip backdoors, Walton slipping a deft bounce to him at the baseline; or the guards picking, feinting, then launching themselves inside leaving frustrated opponents a half step behind and out of the play. Because the center passed, everyone was encouraged to keep moving without the ball. The passing game was infectious. It was no coincidence that Portland led the NBA in assists, and Walton led all centers in that category. For the basketball lover, perhaps the more old-fashioned basketball lover, the Portland style of basketball is a delightful blend of the patterned, pick and roll, give and go type of game that predominated in the forties and fifties with just enough of modern "in your face," school yard battle of ego one-upmanship to be unpredictable. There was no more enjoyable team in the NBA to watch than the Portland Trail Blazers.

Part of the reason Walton was so magnificent on the court during the 1976–77 season was that he had diffused two personal issues—his long hair was gone and his clothes were "presentable." Most important, however, politics for the first time seemed no longer such a pressing issue for Bill Walton. The Patty Hearst situation was resolved and, of course, Richard Nixon was gone. In addition many of the positions Walton had long favored concerning issues such as ecology, the nonproliferation of nuclear energy plants, and the Indian self-help movement were growing increasingly popular in Oregon. Walton seemed emotionally free from intense political entanglements and other hassles that had marked his career from the very beginning.

Walton grew up in La Mesa, California, a bedroom suburb a few miles east of downtown San Diego, one of four children in a sports-minded family. His father, Ted, is a district supervisor in the San Diego Public Welfare Department, who by all accounts put in yeomanlike work

The Pride of Portland

ferrying his number two son through a succession of basketball leagues in the city; in one summer alone it is reported that young Bill Walton played in five leagues. Walton's height, though certainly extraordinary, isn't wholly surprising when you consider his father is 6'4" and his mother is 5'10". Older brother Bruce, who attended UCLA on a football scholarship and played two seasons with the Dallas Cowboys, eventually grew to be 6'6", 280 pounds. Size ran in the family. And it was the early growth spurts of young Bill that led to his first knee trouble; trouble that required the first of many leg operations when he was 15 years old. The growth spurts also ended Walton's professed desire of playing against "bigger kids, 'cause it's more challenging."

After attending Roman Catholic parochial schools for grammar school and junior high school, Walton transferred to La Mesa's Helix High. Hobbled by his leg problems, primarily the beginning of the tendonitis which has made it painful for him to play ever since, Walton concentrated on exercises to improve his coordination and agility. And he worked on his passing. "I couldn't run very well so there was no way I could stay with everybody on the fast breaks. All I did was get the rebound, made the quick pass, and watch everybody go. I got pretty good at it, I did it so much. And I sort of enjoyed standing back there, watching our guys destroy everybody at the other end of the court."

Destroy is the perfect word to describe Helix High's performance with Bill Walton as center. Midway through his junior year "Mount Helix," as Walton was then nicknamed, experienced his last high school defeat—in fact his last defeat for the next 142 games (the streak finally broken by Notre Dame in Walton's senior year in college).

During his senior year in high school Walton averaged 29 points and 22.4 rebounds per contest, and was selected an All-America in both his junior and senior years. In addition he was an outstanding student, finishing twenty-ninth out of a class of 575. Gordon Nash, his high school coach, explained Walton's academic performance this way: "Bill is an excellent student and not necessarily because he's a super brain. It's because he's a *super achiever*. I've known him to spend all weekend on an English paper he wanted to get an A on."

The incursions on his private life, which came to disturb and upset Walton so much in later years, also began in high school. Walton, while a senior in high school, took a friend to a concert in San Francisco and found when he returned home that his trip had wound up being reported in the paper. "I can't do anything," he told coach Nash, "without reading about it in the paper." It was the first reported incident of Walton's treasured privacy being broken.

Deluged by over 110 college scholarship offers, Walton decided to join his brother Bruce at UCLA. Another freshman, Keith Wilkes, joined Walton and together they formed the heart of yet another UCLA college dynasty. A scholarship, though clearly a certainty from the time he was a freshman or sophomore in high school, did not go unappreciated by Walton. Later he remarked: "My parents weren't poor, and I never wanted for anything, but they weren't rich and they've worked hard all their lives to get by. They're sending my sister through college but if their sons didn't get athletic scholarships, we wouldn't all have gotten to go."

After his outstanding freshman season (18.1 pts. and 16 rebounds) Walton began his sophomore year with a series of superlative performances that gained him an enormous amount of national exposure and ended forever his desire for a truly private life. Even as a sophomore the recurring tendonitis necessitated a half hour of heat treatment on his knees before every practice or game and a half hour of ice afterward. But even the bad knees didn't stop the pro coaches and scouts from beginning a three-year stint of salivating over the "big redhead." Jack Ramsay, then coach of a weak 76er team that was in the course of a 30–52 losing season, was quoted in *Sporting News:* "There is a center in college right now who can help us, Bill Walton, but he's only a sophomore." One can imagine the sadness with which Ramsay delivered the foregoing. All he needed was patience, his time was coming.

Walton's play on the court was often overshadowed by his political activities and statements. In a protest over the mining of Haiphong Harbor during his sophomore year Walton, complete with suitably strident placard, was arrested and his picture was flashed across the country. On another occasion Walton stated: "I wouldn't blame the blacks for any steps they took, violent or nonviolent, to get where they should be." Walton was, of course, not saying anything that millions of his peers weren't saying in living rooms and college campuses all over the country. His statements, or rather that he, an athlete, was making them at all, reflected some of the great changes going on in the athletic world. Jack Scott, later a friend of Walton's, commented at the time: "What Walton's experience [protests, etc.] shows us is that the athletic world is more heterogeneous than before. I think the athlete should represent the feelings of the nonathlete and the society at large. That's what I think Bill Walton is doing."

On the court, UCLA marched to a sixth consecutive NCAA championship during Walton's sophomore year. Walton averaged 21.1 points and 14.1 rebounds per game, and was selected College Player of the Year. In the NCAA tournament he shot an astounding .683 (though that was below his amazing season-long mark of .704) and personally destroyed the Florida State Seminoles in the championship game by scoring 24 points and grabbing 20 rebounds. But UCLA only won the game by a margin of five points (81–76) and Walton was morose after the game. "I'm not that elated because we didn't play that well. Florida is an excellent team, but we didn't dominate the game the way I know we can. If we had played our game it would have been different. No excuses, but I don't like to back into things, I like to win convincingly. I felt like we lost it." Incredulous newsmen in the locker room couldn't believe that Walton was sincere about his feelings. They continued to pepper the dejected Walton, understandably assuming that he would snap out of it and realize he'd just participated in an achievement that millions of basketball players and their fans dream about. Instead Walton eventually snapped, "I've answered enough silly questions," and refused to utter another word to the press. It was characteristic of Walton's career that what should have been his moment of greatest triumph became a terribly disappointing and anger-producing situation.

Part of the problem was Walton's striving for perfection. There has never been anyone who plays any harder or works any harder than Walton. When they played together at UCLA, Swen Nater said, "Walton works harder during practices and during games than anyone else on our team." He was in a class with the hardest-working basketball players ever, including the likes of Dave Debusschere, Al Attles, John Havlicek, K. C. Jones, Willis Reed, and Bill Russell. Walton went full bore, night after night, playing with enormous concentration and fire. His eyes seemed to glaze over when his intensity rose then receded into his head like tiny points of pure energy capable of preternatural feats of physical prowess.

A game during his senior year best illustrated Walton's capacity to "get up." It was a rematch with Notre Dame, one week after the Irish had broken the 88-game UCLA win streak and Walton's personal 147-game unbeaten streak at South Bend. In the losing game Walton had played with a back brace, allowing him to make his first appearance in 12 days after falling hard to the floor in a rough game against Washington State. The hostile crowd, packed into the brand-new Notre Dame Convocation Center, screamed and thundered throughout the game, seeming to unnerve the Bruins who lost an 11-point lead with three and a half minutes to play. Notre Dame guard Dwight Clay, a low percentage shooter the entire year, nailed a long jump shot and the Bruins lost 71–70. A quietly seething John Wooden tersely stated after the game that "we'll get a better measure about the two teams after next Saturday's game." In the polls the next week UCLA lost its number one ranking for the first time in seven seasons.

Walton's preparation for the encounter was especially intense. "Walton's been psyching himself all week for this game," said Larry Farmer, a three-year varsity starter who remained at UCLA as assistant coach of the junior varsity. "He gets like this only a few times a year, but when he does he's unstoppable. He wants it, and don't let anybody fool you. The whole team wants it, too."

Banners at Pauley Pavilion on game night demonstrated UCLA's impertinence toward anyone brash enough to usurp the Bruins' role as best team in the land. "Hail, Mary, Full of Grace," proclaimed one sign, "Notre Dame Is Second Place!"

Walton led the Bruins onto the floor for their pregame warm-ups. After the layup drills as a unit, the players began their individual shooting. Walton was taking 20-foot hooks and driving to the basket.

"Everyone could sense his intensity," said freshman Marques Johnson. "It spread so rapidly we couldn't believe it. . . . You would have thought this was the finals of the NCAA."

The Pride of Portland

With five minutes left in the game Walton fouled out, leaving a trail of havoc behind him. The final score was 94–75. Walton shot 16 for 19 to score 32 points and added 11 rebounds. He ripped apart All-American John Shumate so thoroughly that the game was never really in doubt.

Digger Phelps, Notre Dame's coach, said, "They tell me that he practices harder than most ballplayers perform. I guess we got him angry by beating UCLA back there [South Bend]. Whatever the pros pay him won't be enough. He dominated every phase of play. How many times do you see that kind of performance? He scored thirty-two points without ever getting to the free-throw line. I think we discovered his weakness. He doesn't draw fouls well."

Walton after the game: "We like pressure. I know I thrive on it. And I even like hostile crowds. They make me want to play harder."

In his junior year at UCLA Walton continued his heroics of the year before. But with his great play came increasingly frequent demands on his time from the press. And increasing clashes. "I don't think I'm all that important. I don't want to be made into a cardboard cutout, and I don't want people to be disappointed when they find out I'm something other than what they want me to be." Walton, who lived off campus, didn't have a telephone "because I don't want to be bothered." Increasingly professional scouts were also around in addition to the press. Walton referred the scouts to Sam Gilbert, a UCLA alumnus who handled the negotiations with the pros for Kareem Abdul-Jabbar among many other UCLA athletes. The pros by this time all felt the way Jack Ramsay had the year before; Walton was clearly the most attractive collegian since Jabbar. Bill Fitch, coach of the expansion Cleveland Cavaliers, said that to get Walton "I might schedule twenty games a year in LaCosta, California."

College opponents would just as soon have seen him depart. Washington Coach Marv Harshman, after seeing his team eaten up by Walton: "I kinda wish Alcindor was back." USC coach Bob Boyd goes even a little further: "He may well be the best basketball player . . . ever."

UCLA meanwhile continued to play superb basketball, setting a new NCAA record for consecutive victories (breaking the Bill Russell led San Francisco team record set in the fifties) by defeating Notre Dame at South Bend by a score of 82–63.

Walton continued to be annoyed with the press, particularly when they singled him out repeatedly, rather than attributing UCLA's victories to "team ball." To one reporter he said: "I wish you wouldn't write about how I match up against other centers. Because it's not Bill Walton who wins, but UCLA." Ted Green, in an article in *Sporting News*, quoted Walton saying: "I'm not a public person in any sense of the word. I think the media perceived me in a certain way—always writing me up as a super star. I mean UCLA could play without me and win."

Walton's modesty seemed curiously naïve from someone who has such confidence in his own abilities, but nonetheless genuine. Increasingly he was asked about comparisons between himself and Jabbar, a question that never failed to annoy him. "Listen, nobody who knows basketball compares me to him. He's the greatest." Walton walked out on the sportswriter who asked that question. But of course, his protestations to the contrary, it was—and is—a comparison well worth making. No less a basketball expert than Jerry West stated during Walton's junior year that "I really think Walton will be a better pro than Jabbar."

The pressures continued to mount on Walton during his junior year, often imposed by himself as he struggled to discover just what he really wanted, what he really felt. At one point he said, "I'm not convinced playing pro will make me happy." Another time that "it would be nice to have a lot of money but I know a lot of people with lots of money who are unhappy. My idea of living is to enjoy life. That's all. Life is too short to feel any other way." Besides, he added, "I couldn't spend that much in a lifetime anyway."

But it was not just money that was bothering him. He also was questioning his own fans' reactions to his play. Green reported this Walton reaction: "How can they go stark raving mad over us? What do we do that's so important? Put a round ball in a basket. I wonder what's inside their brains?" In *The Lonely Heroes* Walton is quoted saying: "Some people have weird priorities. They'll build places like Pauley Pavilion while other people are starving. Adults will go berserk at our games." But the continual self-questioning and self-analysis which Bill Walton (along with the rest of his introspective generation) put himself through seemed to have no effect upon his play. Nor did the increasing pressure from the professionals to declare "hardship" and leave UCLA to enter the NBA directly after his junior year. "When the time comes to play pro, I'll be able to get the money. But money and material things don't matter that much to me." Sometimes he even sounded like that competitive fire, that lust for victory, which is so crucial to athletic success at a high level, may have been waning. "If winning or losing a basketball game is the worst thing that happens to me I'll be all right."

But as UCLA marched to another championship, Walton remained, perhaps paradoxically, as competitive as ever. Before a tournament game with Indiana, Green reported that Walton, irritated that Indiana might employ stalling tactics against UCLA, said: "If Indiana tries a slowdown tell them to save their plane fare." Indiana did

The Pride of Portland

try the slowdown, by the way, and did lose their plane fare.

But Indiana wasn't the only team to lose its plane fare after tangling with Walton. His performance in the NCAA tournament in 1973 surpassed his previous year's show. In the first game against Arizona State Walton hit on 13 of his 18 shots, then in two slowdown games against San Francisco and Indiana he went four for seven, and seven for 12. That set the stage for the finals when Walton produced the greatest game in modern collegiate history. Against an excellent Memphis State team Walton took 22 shots, made 21, and crushed the second best team in the country 87–66. He scored 44 points in all and shot an ungodly .758 from the field over the course of the tournament. Again he was Player of the Year and again MVP of the NCAA tournament. But after the performance Walton would only say: "I'm in a hurry to go see some friends. Excuse me, please." Gene Bartow, the losing coach, made things a mite easier for the press: "He's a super, super athlete. You just can't realize the strength he has. We wanted to force him out, but he just bumps, bumps, and keeps on going inside. He's too strong to force out. He's the greatest college player of all time."

The "friends" Walton was headed to see turned out to be Irv Kosloff and Don DeJardin, the owner and general manager of the Philadelphia 76ers, who were waiting with what was later reported to be a $2-million contract offer, an offer that had already been made to Sam Gilbert, Walton's financial adviser.

But next day at a news conference Walton also "reaffirmed" for the media his decision to stay at UCLA and his reasons:

"I am not playing pro basketball next year. I have decided there is plenty of time left to earn a living, but now is my time to be a young man. All the attention and the publicity and the financial bonanzas are not for me or my life. I don't need any reasons for coming back. I'm here and that's it. Money has not been a factor—I wish people would understand that. I dig change for the better, but I'm not changing now. My six months as a basketball player are over. Now I get six months to be a human. I want to get away and get some reality into my life."

Walton spent the summer between his junior and senior years acquiring two new disciplines: Transcendental Meditation and vegetarianism. He returned to campus after a vacation spent in the outdoors which included a bicycle trip in the Sierras. Somewhat surprisingly, despite the new vegetarian diet, he gained weight, adding 15 pounds to a frame that was already deceptively strong.

It is interesting to note that many people have underestimated Walton's superior strength—perhaps because vegetarians aren't *supposed* to be strong. Oscar Robertson, after seeing Walton play, was one who thought he might have some problems with strength: "I don't think he's going to come in and take the pros apart, the way a lot of people seem to. His game is more finesse than power and that'll be a big difference for him when he comes up against all the strong people in the pros." Tom Meschery, an assistant coach with the Blazers, was "depressed" the first time he saw Walton. Meschery described him as a man "Washington Irving could have used as a model for Ichabod Crane. I had seen skinny basketball players before in my twelve years in pro sports. There was Wayne Hightower, whose cheeks were so sunken that he always appeared to be sucking on a straw. And there was Bill Russell, whose skin was like children's shirts worn thin at the elbows."

But Walton's appearance was deceptive. Sportswriter

The Pride of Portland

Marty Bell, who has followed Walton since college, had doubts about the big man's strength too, until he saw Walton deal physically with the immense Darryl Dawkins. "Now I can attest to his strength. He gave Dawkins as much as he got." The fact that Walton in both college and the pros continually managed to get positioned down low, where everyone who is a center wants to be but few end up, was testament to his power. He went where he wanted to on the court.

With a stronger and by all indications happier Bill Walton UCLA fans expected another repetition of the previous two undefeated 30–0 national championship seasons. It wasn't to be. In a nationally televised game Walton led UCLA over highly touted North Carolina State, decisively winning his battle with State's 7'4" Tommy Burleson as the Bruins won 84–66. The Bruins kept winning until the 88-game streak was finally broken by Notre Dame, but opponents were concentrating more and more energy on Walton, pushing his teammates further to the perimeter and making it more difficult to get the ball to Walton inside. In February UCLA lost consecutive night road games to Oregon and Oregon State, shocking the basketball world. They eventually won the Pacific Eight championship by a mere one-game margin. In the NCAA, UCLA just squeaked by a small Dayton team in three overtimes. After qualifying for the NCAA finals by defeating San Francisco, UCLA met North Carolina State in a rematch of the earlier season battle. Walton played magnificently, scoring 29 points and grabbing 18 rebounds, but UCLA's streak of seven consecutive NCAA championships was stopped in double overtime. (State went on to defeat Marquette for the national championship.)

Walton's final season was statistically the worst of his three years. He scored 90 fewer points than in his junior year and had 108 fewer rebounds. For the first time he did not win the Player of the Year award, though he was, of course, a first team All-America for the third straight year, joining Oscar Robertson, Jerry Lucas, Bill Bradley, Lew Alcindor, and Pete Maravich as the only men ever to be so honored. Walton in his career totaled 1,767 points, second only in UCLA history to Alcindor; he also shot .651 from the field, breaking Lew's .639 record, and totaled 1,370 rebounds, breaking Alcindor's record of 1,367. He was an academic All-American as well during his junior and senior years and graduated from UCLA with a degree in history. In addition, he won the prestigious Sullivan award as the nation's top amateur athlete in 1973.

As the 1973–74 NBA season drew to a close Dick Motta, then coach of the Chicago Bulls, was quoted as saying certain NBA teams were maneuvering into position—presumably by losing—to get Walton. "The rumor is that some teams in the last year are doing their best to finish last so they can get the draft rights to Walton." The next day after the story broke Motta denied the whole thing. Meanwhile rumors persisted that Walton would only play in a "warm climate." San Diego, with Wilt Chamberlain as coach, got the draft rights to Walton for the ABA. Philadelphia and Portland, the teams with the worst records in the eastern and western divisions of the NBA, flipped a coin for the right to draft Walton. Portland won the flip—to collective sighs from NBA owners who thought there was almost no chance Walton would play in Philadelphia.

Each team sent signed bids to Sam Gilbert. At this time Walton's father, Ted, told his hometown San Diego *Tribune*: "Bill has certain firm ideas about where he wants to play, the kind of organization he wants to play with, and, of course, the way he wants to live. Overriding to him is the way to live.... We're not participating in an auction. One offer will be accepted from each league, and that will

The Pride of Portland

be it. The decision will be solely Bill's. He's a man. He has a mind of his own. I think many people have found that out."

The ABA desperately needed Bill Walton, figuring that he would be the galvanizing presence both on and off the court that Joe Namath was for the old AFL; the lynch pin around which an entire league could coalesce. The San Diego offer was something around $2.5 million, a figure, it was rumored, that would require most of the teams in the league to contribute to, if it were to be met. While Walton decided, the ABA signed three of the top collegians in the country, Marvin Barnes of Providence, Len Elmore of Maryland, and Bobby Jones of North Carolina, further strengthening the credibility of their league.

Walton, of course, signed with Portland, accepting a contract somewhere around $2 million, approximately $500,000 less than the ABA offer. Headlines around the country screamed: Watch Out for Portland! ! a team that already had two highly touted young all-stars in Geoff Petrie and Sidney Wicks.

After four years of dreary last-place finishes the Portland Trail Blazers and their loyal fans (attendance had risen steadily during the team's first four seasons despite the team's continued poor play) finally had hope for a "big" year. Harry Glickman stated: "Our goal for the year is to reach the playoffs." Lenny Wilkens, the new coach, in a burst of optimism, decided that his 37-year-old legs still had enough bounce in them (and they did; for a while Wilkens led the league in assists and played the entire season with a good deal more distinction than the rest of the team) to run up and down NBA courts a few thousand more times. "Ichabod Crane" himself arrived at Portland's training camp a full 20 pounds lighter than he played during his senior year at UCLA. At 215 he was as light as he had been since high school, the weight loss the result of a stricter type of vegetarian diet adopted during the summer.

To Meschery, however, it didn't matter. Nothing did after that first intersquad practice: "I remember elbowing Lenny as if I was trying to keep him out of the pivot. 'Did you see that?' I said. 'Or that?' My elbows didn't seem to matter to Lenny. He was smiling."

According to Meschery, "From the very beginning the rest of the players on the Portland Trail Blazers knew Bill Walton was special. A quick pass to the open cutter, a blocked shot that doesn't sail out of bounds but falls into the hands of a teammate, a controlled tip after a miss. All of these skills do not go unnoticed. It may be difficult for veterans to accept great rookies at first, but they cannot deny talent when they see it." The veterans who formed the core of the team were high scorers Sidney Wicks and Geoff Petrie, steady John Johnson, and two youngsters: Lloyd Neal and Larry Steele. The team had finished fifth in the Pacific Division of the NBA the previous season, last for the fourth consecutive year. Now everyone's expectations were high.

In his first professional game, at home against the Cleveland Cavaliers, Walton scored 18 points, fouled out in the final minutes, but led Portland to a 131–129 victory. After the first few weeks of the new season Walton demonstrated that he could play with great finesse and intensity. Three Portland players were averaging above 20 points per game. Walton was scoring in the mid teens early in the season, seeming to bear out Wick's observation that Walton didn't need to score for Portland to be successful, and he led the league in rebounding and blocked shots. (Jabbar, normally a leader in each category, slammed and broke his hand against a basket support after being poked in the eye and as a result was not playing.) But even with Walton's performance the team got off to a slow start despite a four-game win streak, the longest in the team's history. On November 3 Walton broke his little finger, the first of over 25 major injuries he would suffer as a Portland Trail Blazer.

Later, when painful bone spurs in his left ankle forced him to the sidelines, rumors of malingering seeped through the league, and many Portland fans seemed to feel that Walton could—or at least should—be playing. Walton's devotion to natural foods and the care of his own body became, instead of personal positions he had every right to hold, controversial issues upon which fans and sportswriters held a wide range of opinions. At this same time other problems came up which quickly overshadowed the bone spurs.

Reports hit the newspapers that friends and house mates of Walton's, Jack and Micki Scott—longtime social critics and sports activists—were somehow involved in the flight of Patty Hearst from federal authorities. Walton claimed that he was being harassed and later showed proof supporting a contention—widely thought to be a paranoid delusion when Walton first made the claim—that his phone was being tapped by the FBI. Suddenly the long-haired, headband-wearing, bearded Walton became the object of an enormous amount of scorn from people who seemed to be saying, "I told you so, all those hippies are anti-American." Walton found himself a symbol, for both sides, in an intense, bitter, political struggle between liberals and conservatives. Accustomed to being a hated Goliath on the basketball court, Walton now found himself even more highly visible as a "pinko." The sports director of a Portland radio station (according to Jack Scott in his book *Walton*) issued a ringing denouncement of Walton which accurately reflected the passionate distaste for Walton that was alive around the country. "Ever since his undergraduate days at UCLA Bill Walton has demonstrated to all those who care to listen that his political leanings match the color of his hair: red! He is socialistic in his thinking, and he is proud of it. There's a sticker we've seen on the windshields of many cars, it says: America, Love It or Leave It! Bill Walton obviously does not believe in the former . . . so we suggest he try the latter."

This kind of hysteria was bound to affect anyone, but especially an essentially shy 21-year-old. Tom Mescherey said that Walton was "depressed" at this time and went on to say: "I can't remember, in the history of sport, any athlete who was beset by so many problems. How could it not have affected him? In one year I watched an enthusiastic and happy young man go sullen. More and more he withdrew from the inner workings of the basketball team. He would answer questions politely, at times allow himself to be drawn into arguments or small talk. But he had no heart for it. It is somehow more pathetic to see a man Bill Walton's size slowly losing enthusiasm."

Yet, on the court, Walton continued to show flashes of brilliance. Against Phoenix on January 28 he had 11 assists, 13 rebounds, 12 points, and seven blocked shots to lead Portland to a victory. Other players continued to be impressed by his play. Dave Cowens described Walton as a "great passer," and John Havlicek commented that "he's got a great instinct for making things happen."

Along with Walton's problems, the team experienced internal difficulties. Wicks and Petrie were apparently not getting along, and both began to have doubts about Walton. In an article in the Spokane *Chronicle* Petrie offered some quiet criticism of Walton, which he later backed off from. "I do not question his ability or talent. He's got as much as anybody who ever played. But for anyone to be successful he has to be dedicated to whatever he's doing. I think before he's successful he's going to have to make

The Pride of Portland

some changes in his life." The next day Petrie said that he "didn't think he'd had anything really negative to say about Bill. I really agree with a lot of what Bill says [politically]. I feel just as strongly as he does. I think his choice of words is very poor sometimes. He says things and doesn't realize their implications."

The frustration of having such high expectations for the season and then having those expectations so quickly dashed affected everyone. Lenny Wilkens, to his credit, never joined those criticizing Walton. "I don't blame Bill in any way. When you're hurt, you just can't play."

The final blow of Walton's rookie year occurred on February 18 when his left ankle was put in a walking cast. It was announced that his season was over. Walton played in only 35 games and was fully healthy for only 17. Despite everything else that happened during Bill Walton's rookie year in the NBA, injuries (he missed 47 games) were the real story of the season.

Walton, in an interview with UPI, summed up his season and at the same time squelched rumors that he would give up professional basketball. "I'm only twenty-two, and that is a young age for a professional athlete. I am looking forward to a long career in the NBA. I love basketball. I love to play it, and I plan to play it for a long time. I think I can help the Portland Trail Blazers. I believe they think I can be an asset to the team. . . . The people in Portland and the fans in the NBA have not yet seen me play my best basketball . . . they must remember I have been hurt."

There was every reason to believe that the 1975–76 NBA season would mark the emergence of Bill Walton as a superstar. The one major problem most experts agreed Walton suffered from during his rookie year—lack of weight—was clearly no longer a problem. Walton arrived at training camp weighing 251 pounds. For Portland's

The Pride of Portland

"never" team—never in the playoffs, never a winning season, never even a 40-victory season, never the same coach for two seasons in a row—this was going to be a year of firsts. The starting lineup looked set with Wicks and Lloyd Neal alongside Walton and fabulous rookie Lionel Hollins complementing shooter Geoff Petrie with speed and defense. Two excellent substitutes, Larry Steele at guard and small forward, and John Johnson, a starter the previous season, at shooting and power forward. But as quickly as the hopes rose, that was how quickly they were squashed.

During training camp Walton tripped over the sprinkler on his West Linn lawn and broke the toe of his right foot. Slowed for a few weeks, he then, in the second exhibition game, suffered an eye injury which required a trip to the hospital. Coming back home, his car was rammed by a motorist who had run a red light and Walton's legs were badly bruised. In early December, Walton discovered that he had a hairline fracture of the left wrist. Despite a cast, he decided to play against Washington anyway. He dislocated two fingers of his right hand during the second quarter and was out again.

An incredulous Harry Glickman reported to the press that Walton could "play with either injury but not with both." Glickman also found it necessary to defend Walton. "There's been absolutely no problem with Bill in any other way. His attitude has been great and he's played hard when he's healthy."

And when Walton returned to action, further controversy erupted. The Atlanta Hawks, for example, planned a big promotion for a game against Portland featuring Walton as the attraction. But after a raft of phone calls along the lines of "I wouldn't buy tickets to see that commie bum," the ticket-selling promotional campaign was canceled.

The Pride of Portland

After suffering through the worst start in the team's history—Portland, during the month of January, for the first time finally began to show promise. A seven-game win streak was put together at the end of January and the beginning of February and Walton's play improved dramatically. The team's record moved up to 23–28 until disaster struck on February 8 when Walton suffered a stress fracture of the right leg. He didn't return until March 14.

Walton had improved his statistics over his rookie year by season's end from 12.8 points per game to 16.1 and had hauled down 240 more rebounds. But still he had missed 31 games. Clean living and hard work were not paying off for Walton.

But an athlete with Walton's competitiveness wouldn't easily accept failure. He analyzed his problems and made some decisions. According to Jack Scott, one of the most important was to "cool it" on the political side of his activities. "After the first two seasons, Bill wanted to do everything he could to have a successful season, knowing that his opportunity to effect social change would only exist if he established himself as an athlete. He realized that if he chose to make a stand on too many issues, he'd get labeled as a weirdo or kook." So Walton decided to recede slightly from the limelight and concentrate more on his basketball. And this season he would form a friendship with someone who wanted to do the exact same thing.

Maurice Lucas, a fellow vegetarian and limelight-avoider, became Walton's closest friend on the team. The two had met as juniors in college in St. Louis during the NCAA championships. They apparently spent an evening together and found they had a good deal in common. Then Lucas left Marquette after his junior year to go hardship and join the pros, and Walton continued his brilliant collegiate career. Now three years later Lucas wound up in

The Pride of Portland

Portland. The night before the 1976–77 preseason practices began Walton and Lucas spent a long evening together, presumably discussing the prospects for the upcoming season. According to Jack Scott, Walton returned home that evening extremely excited and optimistic, repeating over and over how good the team could be and what a pleasure it would be to play with Lucas. "I'm pumped. I'm pumped. Luke is great. I just wish the season started tomorrow. We're going to have a damn good team."

Their friendship has apparently strengthened each other off the court and on, and very probably was the crucial factor in cementing the unique brand of unselfish basketball that later would lead Portland to an NBA championship.

Walton's play during the championship season was all that had been predicted for him when he left UCLA. Rave reviews poured in from around the NBA. Larry Brown, the Denver Nugget coach: "I've never seen a player who was more crucial to his team's success than Walton." Gene Schue, former coach of the Philadelphia 76ers: "Walton is the best basketball player for a big man in the history of the game." Paul Silas described him as the "premier center in basketball." Norm Van Lier of the Chicago Bulls said: "I've played against them all, including Wilt, but Bill Walton's more mobile and can do more things. He allows Portland to cut off everything you want to do."

Finally it had all come together, and Bill Walton was obviously enjoying himself as he never had before in professional basketball. Bill Livingston, a sportswriter for the Philadelphia *Inquirer*, caught the essence of Walton's play and attitude during the course of the 1976–77 season with this paragraph: "He is a galvanic presence speeding up and down, joining the give and take of a practice session, joking, taking as much or more as he gives, laughing—and

The Pride of Portland

thoroughly, absolutely, unmistakenly enjoying himself. It is a rare and distinctive portrait—this visceral love for the game at which he makes a living."

At the same time that the team was winning, Walton and the fans of Portland found a mutual admiration society. "The best thing about our fans," said Walton, "is that as hard as they cheer for us, they almost never get abusive to the visiting players." Now instead of doubts about the Portland area Walton said simply: "I love it here." And the response to Walton and the team from the Portland area became a phenomenon known around the country as Blazermania, prompting Larry O'Brian, the NBA commissioner, to say after the championship game: "The spirit of the community and the entire state was the most impressive outpouring of support for a team that I've ever seen."

Then came the 1977-78 season which would end with Portland and Bill Walton involved in the most bitter controversy of Walton's career.

10

MAURICE LUCAS

WHEN THE NAME Maurice Lucas is mentioned, most basketball fans think: intimidator. And then an *indelible* picture comes to mind, a crystal-clear memory of two enormous men, fists clenched, arms raised in classical boxing position of readiness, eyes blazing at one another with almost maniacal anger. There was something riveting in the confrontation between Darryl Dawkins, the biggest, strongest, and certainly meanest-looking dude in the NBA, and the Blazers' perpetually scowling Maurice Lucas. That one frozen moment told basketball fans—and fellow players—that Maurice Dorand Lucas had come to win, and that nothing, not even the prospect of an awful physical confrontation with the immense Dawkins, would deter him from that goal.

If that nationally televised bout confirmed a conception already widely held in basketball circles—that Lucas was the ultimate enforcer, a man always ready to defend and to fight, for his position ("I don't want anybody in my territory") at the slightest hint of attempted physical intimidation directed at him or his teammates—it would get no support from its creator. No fuel will be laid on this smoldering fire; off the court Lucas' "whole life is a search for peace within." The harsh, grimacing visage on the court calms perceptibly off the court, the eyes soften, the features smooth, the entire countenance, if not beatific, at least passive and clearly peaceful. The voice which rails on the court at officials is quiet, almost inaudible. The player who seemed continually on the edge of a violent outburst, whose temper is hair-triggered, is a man who is thoughtful, controlled, temperate, and gentle; a man, according to Marty Bell, who profiled Lucas in *Sport* magazine, possessing "restraint and maturity that seems beyond his 25 years."

"My whole life is a search for peace within," said Lucas. "I know that phrase is tossed around a lot today. What it means to me is accepting the situation around oneself, accepting the things you cannot change, being able to live with them without anger. And then, calmly going about changing the things you have control over. One of the things I can always control is my basketball. I can be as good as I want to be and I'll do anything to be good. I know I'm basically passive and you can't be successful that way. So, to be successful, I have to consciously work myself into a rage. I guess you can say that I live peacefully and I play angry."

The way Lucas played basketball was totally at odds with the rest of his life. He knew that he played best when he was fired up. But in all other phases of his life he headed in the exact opposite direction. Before a game the portrait of Lucas in the locker room was an extraordinary one. He sat in front of his locker and consciously, and quite visibly, worked himself into a playing rage. Suddenly the quiet peace seeker seemed to be breathing fire through flared nostrils, a huge brown lion barely restraining himself from tearing the metal door from its hinges and leaping onto center court in search of the nearest Christian. It was the ultimate in self-psyching acts, Clark Kent without the funny suit, Dr. Jekyll without potions. Perhaps the anger was necessary, perhaps not.

One thing is for sure, whatever Lucas is doing, it worked just brilliantly. Bobby Leonard, coach of the Indiana Pacers, stated flatly that "there isn't a forward in the league better than Lucas. Not George McGinnis, not Julius Erving, not anybody." And Paul Silas, a player who should know, called Luke "the premier power forward in the game. Hayes and Haywood can shoot as well, but Lucas is tougher. He's a very physical player."

According to Jack Ramsay, ideally there are "five things you'd like to have in a power forward—scoring, rebounding, defense, toughness, and speed. Well, in most players you're lucky if you get three. But with Lucas you get all five, plus a man who doesn't make mistakes." His overall assessment of Lucas: "the best power forward in basketball."

The "best power forward in basketball" grew up in the slums of grimy Pittsburgh, Pennsylvania. "We lived in the worst neighborhood in town, of course I didn't know it at the time." His mother, who works with a tuberculosis foundation, brought up Maurice along with an older brother and sister without the help of a husband in the house. Clearly, Lucas' youth was not a childhood of plenty. According to Marty Bell, the first game Lucas played as a child was "hitting supermarkets and fruit markets." Lucas said it was "just as much survival as fun, because we didn't have any money. Some of the guys got caught. I was too sly and too careful for that to happen to me." Maurice was separated from his mother in 1960 at the age of eight when she underwent a serious heart operation from which it took her three years to fully recover. He and his brother and sister "lived with a woman that the hospital sent."

Lucas' memory of childhood poverty accounts for both the careful, serious way he approached his career and the concern he has for kids. "We didn't have a lot of things when I was growing up—like food and clothes—I know what it's like to be poor."

He has worked in a youth program in Portland during the summers running clinics which are partly basketball camps and partly lectures on the value of education, the dangers of drugs, and the value of leadership. One summer more than 7,000 disadvantaged youngsters participated in the Maurice Lucas Summer Youth Involvement Program in Portland. "We take the poor kids and mix basketball clinics with lectures about real problems they got to face every day. There are a few bad kids that I even see during the season. I get a lot of satisfaction out of seeing kids happy." It is a testament to Lucas' sincerity that he even took time during the season to spend time with some special kids. And further testament that his efforts have gotten very little publicity. Lucas felt that the relationship he has with the kids is private, that publicity would infringe on that relationship and ultimately be unfair to the children.

Like many ghetto kids Maurice Lucas played basketball, though it was far from his favorite activity. "I played as a kid, but mostly because my friends wanted to play. I was real little compared to everybody else. What I really wanted to be was a swimmer. I even swam in a state championship for 'Y' teams when I was twelve. I was third or fourth."

As a sophomore at Schenley High School Lucas was a 6' guard on a team coached by Spencer Watkins, a man who demanded great physical conditioning and desire. Lucas now says that with Watkins "if and when we lost it wasn't going to be because of our physical condition or our toughness. We ran the hills around the school, spent a lot of time diving after loose balls, used a lot of forearms."

Between his sophomore and junior years the skinny, somewhat short sophomore had put on weight and a full seven inches. He spent the summer at Temple University in Philadelphia working with younger kids in a community program and playing ball in the famed Sonny Hill League against college and even pro players. He also spent a lot of time eating dorm food, and just kept getting bigger. "It was real embarrassing. We didn't have any money for new clothes and all my pants came up to my knees. So I wore a lot of long socks."

By the time he was a senior in high school there were a raft of college recruiters around, all of whom were willing to buy Lucas a pair or two of appropriate-length pants. In his final season Lucas led Schenley to the state championship and along the way averaged 27.5 points per game and 24.3 rebounds. In one unbelievable game he scored 46 points and had 44 rebounds. Al McGuire described him as "the best prospect I ever saw."

And it was the emotional McGuire who attracted Lucas to Marquette. Actually the man who made the connection was one of McGuire's former players, George Thompson, who while playing for the Pittsburgh Condors of the ABA told Lucas that McGuire was the kind of guy "who hollered at you" and then, Lucas says, "let you holler back at him. That's what I was used to and that's what I wanted. I couldn't make myself into an unemotional ballplayer for some coach."

The relationship between Lucas and the volatile McGuire can be charitably described as stormy. More than a few times national television audiences were treated to scenes of McGuire first staring hard, then shouting at his star center, then seeing the star center yelling right back. Lucas says that "McGuire never picked a fight with me, though. He only fought the guards." No one ever called Al McGuire stupid.

As a freshman (before the frosh were allowed to play varsity sports) Lucas had the best season any Marquette rookie ever enjoyed, averaging 28.6 points and 16.8 rebounds per game. He stepped immediately into the starting lineup as a sophomore and averaged 15.4 points and 10.8 rebounds. After watching the young Lucas help chew up his team, Minnesota coach Bill Museelman observed: "I've never seen a better sophomore anywhere, anytime." He also experienced foul trouble and some temper trouble, fouling out of four games and being tossed from two others because of fighting. At the time Lucas observed: "I don't want to be fouling out so much. I'm no good to the team on the bench. And I don't like sitting beside McGuire anyway."

After his sophomore season Lucas joined the United States team in the World University Games. As a starting forward he averaged 12.5 points and 7.5 rebounds, but most important got an opportunity to travel overseas, particularly in the Soviet Union and Eastern Europe. When he returned, Lucas said: "It was different countries, different people. I got to know a little how they think. I had to use sign language a lot, but I was able to do plenty of talking too. Since I've been overseas I've become a vegetarian. I saw a lot of people who were very healthy, eating little or no meat. I quit eating pork about a year ago and now I eat no meat at all—just fish. I get substitute protein in cheese and other things and I still feel strong. It's not for any religious reasons, it's just a back-to-nature thing."

The new vegetarian returned to Marquette for his junior year and McGuire made this unusual assessment of his star: "If Luke will pay the price, he can be a super player. He has unreal talent, but *he has to become more physical. He's not as rough underneath as he could be.*" Seeing Lucas play now, one wonders how much rougher he could possibly get. Marquette was a powerful team in 1973-74, boasting a starting lineup of Larry McNeil, Lloyd Walton, Bo Ellis, Allie McGuire, the coach's son, and Lucas. Even with all those stars McGuire said of Lucas, "He's our power. As he goes, we go." Playing within McGuire's conservative pattern of offensive play, Lucas averaged 15.8 points and 10.6 rebounds. He also shot .492 from the floor, a pattern of consistently high-percentage shooting that has remained a trademark of his game ever since.

Marquette ended up in the semifinals of the NCAA championships in St. Louis along with UCLA and Bill Walton, North Carolina State with Tommy Burleson and David Thompson, and an unheralded Kansas team. N.C. State defeated Walton and company while Marquette beat Kansas to go to the finals. In the championship game Lucas played marvelously, scoring 21 points and grabbing 13 rebounds, but the combination of Burleson and Thompson accounted for 35 points and 18 rebounds. In addition the volatile McGuire exploded late in the second half and had to be restrained by Lucas and Walton. The result: four technical fouls and a crucial edge for N.C. State. Later a dejected McGuire would admit that "I blew it. I really blew it."

As the season wound down, rumors began that Lucas would consider turning pro by applying for the hardship draft. Jim Chones, a teammate, had done so the previous year and had received a big contract. For Lucas, poor all his life, the financial temptation was enormous. Coach McGuire, who had seen an almost certain NCAA championship team broken up by Chones's decision the year before, could hardly be faulted if he had sounded off, as so many other college coaches had done, about the pros "raiding" the colleges with their "cradle robbing tactics"; but instead the unpredictable Al, a child of poverty himself, gave Lucas his tacit approval, saying: "It doesn't matter whether Luke turns pro early or not. Whatever he does

The Pride of Portland

in life, Luke will be a success. A big success. And on the basketball court he has unbelievable equipment. Everybody will find that out." Lucas himself would only say that "if I didn't get drafted, that'd shake me up. Make me wonder just how good I really am."

Of course Lucas was drafted, second, as a matter of fact, to Marvin Barnes of Providence; after being unable to come to terms with the Chicago Bulls Lucas signed with the Spirits of St. Louis, joining Barnes and Gus Gerard to form an all-rookie front line. Lucas, playing center, started off slowly, then began to come on strong as the season progressed. His coach, Bob MacKinnon, commented: "He's got to be active to be effective. He's not tall enough to just plant himself in the middle against some of the bigger centers. But he's strong and a good shooter. He's also aggressive and you've got to respect him." Lucas himself maintained a realistic though calmly confident attitude: "I learned team offense and team defense at Marquette. I knew I would make mistakes as a rookie, but I also knew I would put it together."

In one 12-game midseason stretch once he started "putting it together" Lucas averaged 19.3 points, 13.9 rebounds, and 5.3 assists per game. He ended up the season averaging just a shade under 19 points per game. Then in the ABA playoffs the Spirits upset the highly favored New York Nets featuring Julius Erving. Lucas went through the Net centers like a giant scythe through a wheat field, thoroughly intimidating them with strength and muscle.

During the series Don Schupak, who negotiated player contracts for the Spirits, finally was able to make up his mind about Lucas. "I couldn't decide whether Maurice was surly or just intense. I've decided that he's intense. He's really serious about being a great pro player. Very serious."

That intensity sometimes translated itself into pushing

The Pride of Portland

and shoving and occasionally outright violence. In a game against the Kentucky Colonels during his rookie year Lucas and Artis Gilmore were banging away at one another, the shorter Lucas most probably the aggressor since Gilmore, to be controlled, must be physically kept as far away from the basketball as possible. Once inside he's deadly. The banging turned to elbowing and finally punches were exchanged; exchanged, that is, until Lucas buckled Gilmore's knees with a "vicious right hand to the nose." Later in the season Lucas and the normally peaceful Julius Erving had a problem which resulted in a black eye for the good doctor. Jim O'Brian, of the New York *Post*, wrote after that incident that "Lucas is fast becoming one of the most feared opponents in the ABA. This is one mean dude."

In his sophomore professional season Lucas was traded from St. Louis to Kentucky for Caldwell Jones. Not before, however, he kayoed Virginia Squires Randy Denton and Jim Eakins in a very brief tussle when Lucas came to the aid of a teammate. Coach Rod Thorn thought it would be an appropriate time to get the angry Lucas out of the game except that Maurice came back to the bench with a smile on his face and said: "Coach, I'm ready now." Thorn left him in the game. "He looked ready to me."

Midway though his second season Lucas was traded to the Hubie Brown–coached Colonels, where he was moved to forward alongside his old adversary Gilmore. Problems immediately arose between Brown and Lucas and the feelings between the two men remain icy, to say the least. Brown says, "We were involved in a lot of arguments, flare-ups, physical confrontations. Naturally it evolved from his own personal style. He had to practice hard with us and participate in a five-man offense, and I don't think he was used to that. He has great tools, but he does a lot of things he shouldn't do out there and that hurts his game."

Lucas responds somewhat more tersely: "Kids who went to Hubie's summer camp used to tell me that Hubie told them Artis Gilmore was a great player and that I was an ass hole. I hate the guy's guts." Looking back at the situation now it is hard to imagine Lucas being too upset with the ultimate result of his difficulties with Brown, for their inability to get along led directly to Luke's arrival with the Blazers.

At the end of the 1975–76 season the NBA and the ABA merged; the Kentucky franchise folded and its players were subject to the dispersal draft. The Chicago Bulls had the first choice in the draft and took Artis Gilmore. The Atlanta Hawks had the second pick. The new Atlanta coach: Hubie Brown. The overwhelmingly obvious second choice in the dispersal draft: Maurice Lucas. Something had to give, since Brown and Lucas were clearly not going to either form a mutual admiration society or even remain comfortably on the same side of the Continental Divide. Jack Ramsay was now the Portland coach and was getting ready to unload Sidney Wicks. Lucas would be the perfect addition to the Blazers, an enormous help for Walton on the boards; in short the perfect power forward. Bob MacKinnon, who was Ramsay's assistant at Buffalo as well as Lucas' coach during his rookie season in the ABA, made the final convincing arguments to Ramsay—that Lucas was coachable, a hardworking ballplayer with an undeserved bad reputation. The Blazers promptly sent Geoff Petrie, who was playing out his option anyway, and Steve Hawes to Atlanta for the second draft choice in the dispersal. Portland then selected Luke, shelled out $300,000, and the making of a championship began. In professional sports parlance the deal was a "steal."

Ramsay said: "I knew he had problems with his previous coach. But all he asked for was to be treated with respect. That's not a hard bargain to keep, is it? When it became

The Pride of Portland

obvious we were going to lose Sidney Wicks, we went looking for a strong forward who could play backup center. And there's no question that, in our system, Luke's a much better ballplayer than Wicks."

At the start of the 1976-77 season most players from the ABA staunchly defended their league, claiming that they knew they could play and "didn't have to show anybody anything." Lucas was just the opposite. He questioned the comparative strength of the ABA with the NBA and concluded that "I definitely have something to prove."

He proved it quickly, teaming with Bill Walton to form the best rebounding and scoring duo in the league. Lucas led the Blazers during the championship season in scoring with 20.2 points per game and was second to Walton in rebounding with 11.4 per game—still good enough to rank ninth in the league overall. Bill Fitch of the Cleveland Cavaliers said at the end of the season: "He was certainly the best power forward in our league. The ABA brought us more physical strength. From the ABA we got George McGinnis, Marvin Barnes, Moses Malone, and Maurice Lucas. And Lucas is the strongest of all."

But despite all the promise, Lucas remained above all a team man. He said, "I shy away from the superstar image. I don't particularly care to be looked upon as a star. Away from the court I'm a pretty quiet guy. I don't like crowds." After the championship game Luke was quoted as saying, "Nobody on the team is a star. We were a team all the way."

"I think what I enjoyed the most was the people all around the country congratulating me and congratulating our team. It's always nicer to go through the summer as a winner than as a loser. Everybody likes a champion. That's human nature and it is important that athletes understand that."

Even in the most climactic, ecstatic time of his life

The Pride of Portland

Maurice Lucas exhibited the kind of control and thoughtfulness that marked his life. He worked hard to set in tune with himself, to understand himself, and to be at peace with that person.

This ability to mentally discipline himself accounted for Lucas' steady consistency over the course of his still young professional career. "Most people see us as physical brutes, but the mental discipline required to play game after game is more crucial than physical talent. That's the hardest thing about the sport, the mental part. We all go through the constant pressure and agony of physical pounding. Just the everyday action of the pounding on your body can make you an old man. You have to deal psychologically with that." But despite that pressure, Lucas said, "I will improve every aspect of my game. There is always room for a player to improve."

11

BOB GROSS

"WHEN I GOT TO PORTLAND I could hardly remember him from his rookie year. I had to look at the films." *(Jack Ramsay)*

When Stu Inman was scouting Lionel Hollins, of Arizona State, in 1975, he traveled to the Sun Devil Classic in which Long Beach State was also playing. At that time, Inman remembered, "I was unaware of Bob Gross." Then a few days later Inman went to scout Lindsay Hairston, of Michigan State, who happened to be playing against Long Beach State in the Cable Car Classic. Recalled Inman, "I was concentrating on Hairston, still pretty much unaware of Gross's existence, when something he did caught my attention."

What caught Inman's attention was a play in which Gross led a Long Beach fast break only to wind up missing an easy layup. The bad miss triggered a Michigan State fast break in the other direction. Lo and behold, the ball went to Lindsay Hairston, who went up for a sure two points—until a flying Bobby Gross came from nowhere to make a spectacular block.

The Pride of Portland

Says Inman: "I turned to the guy next to me and asked, 'That couldn't have been Gross, could it? Why, he was down at the other end just a second ago shooting a layup.' When I realized that Gross made the transition so quickly from offense to defense, I started watching his every move. That's when he started impressing me."

The story of Bob Gross's collegiate and professional basketball life was that nobody noticed him ... until they really started looking hard. Then, with a modicum of basketball knowledge, and a keen eye, they discovered a jewel, a consistent, hardworking, extraordinarily effective basketball player. Dwight Jones, Gross's Long Beach State coach, took awhile to appreciate what he had, then observed, "In ten years of coaching at all levels, Bob Gross is, without a doubt, the most underrated player I have ever seen." Jack McKinney, then an assistant coach with the Milwaukee Bucks, remembered with a laugh the first time he heard Gross's name—at the 1975 NBA draft—when he was selected number 25, surprising an awful lot of people in the NBA. "When the Blazers announced they were taking a Bob Gross of Long Beach State, " McKinney said, "I turned to Wayne Embry (then the Bucks' general manager) and asked, 'Bob Gross? Who's he?' Embry replied, 'Great pick. Portland made a great pick. You'll see.'" McKinney not only saw, he lived to reap both the emotional and financial benefits of Gross's play.

Why is it that so few noticed Bobby Gross? How could he have been so good, and still have been so little recognized? The answer to that question is a combination of where Gross had played and the nature of a typical Bob Gross game.

At Long Beach State where he transferred from Harbor Junior College, via the University of Seattle (where he started on the varsity as a sophomore), Gross played behind two men who received a great deal of publicity, both eventually becoming first-round draft choices in the NBA: Glenn McDonald (Boston) and Clifton Pondexter (Chicago). Long Beach was highly successful 43–9, the seasons Gross played there, but both years the team was on probation with the NCAA and ineligible for postseason play, thereby further limiting the publicity that might naturally have accrued to Gross. Anyway, Bobby Gross didn't even start on the team until he was a senior, averaging only 6.6 points per game his junior year. Even as a senior the school's press guide, a type of publication notorious for overblown praise, described Gross's play as "brilliant all-around consistency"; hardly the kind of drum roll buildup usually given to future pros during their college careers.

From his mystery man days at Long Beach Gross went quietly into the NBA and quickly was buried beneath an avalanche of publicity about Bill Walton's politics and eating habits, and the continuous Sidney Wicks–Geoff Petrie mutual hate society. A rookie averaging 6.8 points per game does not necessarily warrant a *Time* magazine cover story. Not to say that his play wasn't satisfactory; it was, but 'steadily satisfactory'; in short, nobody noticed, including such an astute observer as Jack Ramsay, who "could hardly remember him," when he arrived at Portland. So Bob Gross's timing in terms of choice of place to play for maximum publicity value could hardly have been worse.

Then there was the matter of his style of play, the second contributing factor in Gross's low public recognition quota. Curry Kirkpatrick, in *Sports Illustrated,* called Gross "that prime example of an excellent player toiling for a more than excellent team. Simply he 'fills a role.' While the Waltons, Lucases and Hollinses dominate the statistics and make All-Star teams, Gross spends much of the time, as he says, 'doing what's left over,' " including maintaining a low profile. But as Stu Inman pointed out,

"Though Bob Gross was clearly an underrated player, he was not underrated by our players. They think he's something special." "I've seen games in which I thought Gross played great," said Jack McKinney, "then I look in the box score and the stats don't support what I saw. I think Bobby's greatest contributions to this team can't be translated into statistics."

On the evening of June 3, 1977, Bobby Gross made his big move toward fame and national recognition; not that he would see it that way or do anything other than blush at its suggestion of "stardom." In the crucial fifth game of the NBA championship series against the 76ers, with the teams tied two victories apiece, Gross, in just 25 minutes of play before he fouled out, scored 25 points. He hit ten of 13 from the floor and five of five from the foul line. He had five assists, three steals, and before he fouled out contained the incomparable Julius Erving, who ended up with 37 points, many coming after Gross departed. It was a brilliant all-around display of basketball playing at the highest possible level under the greatest possible pressure. It was THE game of the playoffs and Gross won it. Then in the final he added 24 points on 12 of 16 from the floor to help capture the championship.

Said Jack Ramsey in a postgame interview, Gross "was outstanding. His role was so important to our team's success."

More explicitly, Ramsay defined Gross's attributes as "moving without the ball, keeping the ball alive on the offensive boards, shot blocking, quickness, passing. He is a dedicated team player whose skills are tailor-made for the fast break." Those skills were so varied, according to Stu Inman, that they made Gross "perhaps the most gifted athlete on the Blazer team. In terms of coordination, timing, use of his off hand [left], jumping ability, and quickness, Gross probably is our best." An illustration of Inman's

The Pride of Portland

contention occurred after Gross's rookie year, when he picked up a set of golf clubs, something he had not done since his early teens, and promptly shot a 79.

That sort of ability almost prompted Gross to take up professional baseball as a career. "Baseball would have been easier for me physically," says Gross, "but I think I chose the right sport for my talents."

Further praise recorded after the 1977 title game confirmed Gross did indeed make the right choice. A gracious Julius Erving said of Gross: "He moves so well without the ball that it's hard to keep up with him." A Philadelphia writer echoed the praise: "Bobby tires the man. Why, he tires anybody the way he runs." Walton, in further explanation of Gross's running style, said: "You have to really watch him all the time, and ignore the ball." McKinney summed up the situation in typically accurate fashion: "He's our runner, our distance man. He runs as well as any player in the league." For sheer indefatigability Bob Gross is in the same lofty class as the NBA's all-time roadrunner, John Havlicek; with Hondo's retirement Gross may well stand as the runniest "crazy" in the league.

12

THE GUARDS

*P*ORTLAND'S GUARDS don't have any ego problems. They all believe, really believe, I mean, not just *say* they believe, in substituting. Play with as much intensity as you can, go as hard as you can, then take a rest." *(Marty Bell, sportswriter)*

The Blazers' elite backcourt of Lionel Hollins and Dave Twardzik represented most accurately what Portland's team concept was all about. They sacrificed themselves offensively and defensively in order to submerge their individual games into Jack Ramsay's egoless system.

And this sort of discipline was very difficult for an athlete. Basketball, as learned in school yards and playgrounds, is a game of unleashed ego, of one-upmanship. You got me, now I'm going to get you back. But professional basketball is a game of suppressed ego, of intelligence rather than temperament. After being dazzling individual players through high school and college, players almost have to relearn the game for the pros. They must fit into a system rather than have a system fitted to them. The best teams (like the old Celtic dynasty, or the championship Knicks of a few years ago) are those where the guards are most willing to make this adjustment. The Blazer guards, though very young, were an extraordinarily mature and insightful group of players, and they formed a deadly effective unit that came at the opposition in what seemed like waves of energy and speed.

LIONEL HOLLINS

For the most amply gifted Lionel Hollins there was little trouble adapting to Portland's style of play. Few rookies are ready, upon entering the league, to step into a starting role. Hollins was one. Coach Lenny Wilkins had decided that Hollins deserved a starting position after an excellent exhibition season in 1975, but then right before opening day Hollins had emergency appendectomy surgery and was placed on the disabled list.

For many pro scouts and coaches the success of Lionel Hollins came as quite a surprise. Despite being named to the *Sporting News* 1974–75 first team All-American squad (along with David Thompson, Adrian Dantley, Dave Meyers, Leon Douglas, and John Lucas), Hollins only averaged 16.7 points per game, shot well below 50 percent both during his senior season and for his two-year Arizona State University career, and had played in a run and gun conference that frequently produced all-stars who flopped upon arrival in the NBA. Still Portland didn't have any doubts; they drafted "The Train" first in the 1975 draft. From the first day of practice it was obvious that Hollins was an extraordinarily gifted athlete. That came as no surprise to anyone who had seen him in high school, junior college, or at Arizona State.

At Rancho High School in Las Vegas Hollins won two varsity letters each in basketball, football, and track, earn-

The Pride of Portland

ing all-state and All-America honors in basketball. He was, in addition, the high school player of the year in Nevada his senior year.

He began his college career at Dixie College in St. George, Utah, where again he was all-conference and All-American in basketball. After his second year at Dixie he transferred to ASU, where he was MVP and high scorer for two consecutive years, as well as being a Western Athletic Conference first team selection and an All-American his senior year. In perhaps his finest collegiate game Hollins bombed Oregon's Ron Lee, at that time heralded as the country's outstanding defensive guard, for 30 points.

Hollins' rookie year with Portland was a difficult one despite averaging 10.8 points and 4.6 assists per game and making the all-rookie team. "Last year," Hollins said during his sophomore year, "was a very frustrating experience for me. For one thing, I never played on a team that lost so many games. I thought I'd be starting when the season opened because I'd played pretty well in exhibition games. But then I had to have my appendix out, missed the first two weeks, and didn't really get going good again until the last couple weeks of the season. I didn't know how to play half the guys I was guarding and I had a definite lack of confidence." Still he ended up starting 30 games and appearing in 74 during his rookie campaign. He was one of the few bright spots in a highly disappointing Blazer season.

Then in his sophomore season Hollins emerged, somewhat unexpectedly, as one of the top guards in the NBA. He averaged nearly 15 points a game and led the club in steals and assists. He improved statistically in all departments, upping his field goal percentage from .421 to .432, and his free throw shooting percentage from .721 to .749. He finished seventh in the NBA in steals with an average of 2.18 per contest. In one game against the Boston Celtics

Hollins exploded for 43 points, shooting 20 for 31 from the floor—matching a club record held by Geoff Petrie—and thoroughly demoralizing outstanding defensive guards JoJo White and Charlie Scott.

But it was in the playoffs that Hollins really staked out a position for himself in the NBA. He averaged 17.3 points per game and had more playoff steals, 47, than any other player. In the key Laker series "The Train" hit for 25 points the first game and buried the Lakers with 31 the second—that total being the highest playoff production for any Blazer. Under playoff pressure Hollins was superb. "An 84 percent shooter," Hollins at the time remarked, "sometimes suddenly becomes a 50 percent shooter with six seconds left on the clock and the game on the line. Those last few seconds have a tendency to change percentages very rapidly."

The pressure didn't affect Hollins that way. Example: The third game of the best-of-three series against the Chicago Bulls—probably the toughest, most closely contested series of the entire playoffs—had 30 seconds to run and the Blazers were holding a 100–98 lead and the ball. But Walton, Lucas, and Twardzik had all fouled out and had the game been forced into overtime Portland would have been outmanned. As the 24-second clock wound down Hollins dribbled to the top of the key and calmly pumped in a jumper to clinch the victory. Under pressure, as usual, Lionel Eugene Hollins was tough.

Said Jack Ramsay: "Lionel improved in every category, but most especially in consistency and shot selection. He played with more poise. As a defensive player, he is at or near the top among the NBA's guards."

Dave Twardzik

When Dave Twardzik first joined the Portland Trail Blazers, Bill Walton jokingly greeted him by saying: "You

The Pride of Portland

certainly can't be very good. . . . I've never heard of you."

A lot of people at that time hadn't heard of him. Unheralded is an adjective that may have been created to describe the man the Blazers called, among other things, "Fudd." The general line on Twardzik after he reported for his first Blazer preseason workouts in 1976 would probably have gone something like this: "A little guy who's pretty scrappy on defense, works real hard anyway; no offense at all, not very fast. Lots of guys like him around—a dime a dozen."

Hardly a rave review. If Twardzik had known what many thought, he wouldn't even have unpacked his bags. But he did and he came to stay. After four unimpressive years playing in near total obscurity with the hapless Virginia Squires of the ABA, Dave Twardzik won himself a starting job on a team that became the NBA champions.

How is the next question. The answer: with heart and guts and full bore, total hustle. "He's a coach's player," said Golden State's Al Attles, "and the fans like him too. A lot of coaches really like a Dave Twardzik." In one playoff game, to demonstrate what Attles meant, Twardzik was on the hardwood a total of 15 times, mostly from diving for loose balls or taking charging fouls. No wonder his teammates called him "The Pinball Wizard"—not because of anything to do with the machine, but because of the way he bounced around the court knocking into and off of people. After diving for a loose ball in the waning moments of the meaningless game, Fudd was asked why in the world he would want to do such a thing. "That's the way I play," he said. And for Twardzik there is, apparently, no turning off his effort, no holding back; it is no holds barred or nothing at all.

"Maybe I got all of that [hustle]," Twardzik said, "from going to so many summer basketball camps at a young age. My father was my first coach and he worked me pretty hard on defensive fundamentals. He also taught me to evaluate my game not so much on statistics, but by effort. So now, after each game, I go into the locker room, sit down and ask myself, 'Did you give 100 percent out there tonight?' If I can say yes to that, I can hold my head up and walk out of there."

Twardzik's been holding his head up nice and high ever since high school when he led Middletown Area High to the Class B Pennsylvania State basketball title. Twardzik's position: center. "I guess I learned a lot of my inside moves in high school because I played the pivot. That's right, I was a six-foot-tall center." Needless to say, 6' centers do not generally have scads of recruiters hanging around the house.

Twardzik had plenty of time to himself as a result. He ended up, to his surprise, getting a basketball scholarship. "I was playing in an all-star game in Allentown, Pennsylvania, my senior year in high school, when a coach came up to me and said he was from Old Dominion and would like to fly me down for a visit." According to Wayne Thompson of *The Oregonian,* "Dave had never heard of Old Dominion, but he'd never flown before either." So off he went to Old Dominion University in Norfolk, Virginia, presumably enjoyed his first plane ride, and ended up falling in love with the area and the university.

In three seasons at Old Dominion Twardzik averaged 17.5, 20.3, and 23.4 points per game, placing himself second on the school's all-time scoring list (behind a player who had participated in four years of varsity basketball). He also set a career assist record averaging over ten assists a game for a career total of 880. He still holds records for most free throws made in a season (222) and most free throws attempted in a season (273) as well as most assists in a season (332). He was a first team little All-America selection in his junior and senior years, even set an NCAA tournament record for free throws in one game (24 of 26); still nobody cared. Or almost nobody. His coach was one exception: "Dave's accomplishments and individual statistics are very obvious but his greatest asset is his unselfishness and team play. A player's true value can be judged by what he does for his team and teammates. During his sophomore and junior years, Dave led his team to 42 victories and into the championship game of the 1971 NCAA College Division national tournament. His leadership brought out the best in his team, which is a true indication of an All-America."

Twardzik didn't even consider a professional career as a possibility until his junior year and even then it didn't seem very realistic. But by the time his senior year was completed pro scouts had begun coming around. Twardzik was drafted on the second round of the 1972 draft by the Portland Trail Blazers and was also selected by the Virginia Squires.

"Portland offered about $5,000 more," said Twardzik, "over two years, but I already was settled down with my family in Virginia, and $5,000 didn't seem like enough money to upset them, so I chose Virginia."

With Virginia Twardzik averaged 5.8, 8.7, 13.6, and 7.4 points per game in four seasons, while Virginia played musical chairs with coaches and players. When Virginia folded, Dave Twardzik got a new lease on life, though his indecision about the quality of his "new lease" cost him some money. "I came out here [Portland] one weekend to talk about a contract, and I went home. I came back another weekend, and signed. But the second time back I took a pay cut—I guess as punishment for my indecision. Oh, did I take a pay cut!" Characteristically, Twardzik laughed when telling the story. But money was no laughing matter with Virginia, where paychecks bounced as often as the team's basketballs. "I had two or three that bounced." But the worst thing was that Virginia stopped paying anybody anything on April 4—and business administration major Twardzik was being paid on a twelve-month basis. "We had already played the entire season, and I had been paid five and a half months and they owed me six and a half months more pay. I can't forget it because I never thought in this country you wouldn't get paid for work you'd done. But the worst thing about it was it was the first year of a three-year no-cut contract."

Oh well, a slightly wiser Dave Twardzik signed a Portland contract in June 1976 and immediately began enjoying his basketball again.

Said Twardzik: "Maybe the Old Celtics had it too, and maybe it sounds corny, but this team loves one another ... a kind of love that's hard to explain. Everyone gets along on and off the floor. We just like being with each other. We don't have any guys on ego trips."

And certainly Twardzik was the most unselfish of the unselfish. He fit in perfectly to the Blazer system, providing a degree of steadiness and court sense that was lacking in other years. "He's made for our system," said Bill Walton. "He's very good at moving without the ball and getting himself open on the baseline. We have a lot of good passers on this team and if a player moves well and gets open, he will get the ball." "The Polish Prince" for his part couldn't agree more. "I think my game has been basically the same for every team I've played for. But I get more opportunities with the Blazers because we have a center who is not only willing to give up the ball, but is the best in the business at hitting the open man. That's been the big difference for me."

Walton, however, is not the only one willing to give up the ball. In one game during the 1977 season Twardzik stole the ball from the Celtics' JoJo White and was heading for an uncontested layup when he spotted Lloyd Neal hustling down court to trail the play just in case. "I thought to myself," said Twardzik, "that Lloyd ought to get something out of such an effort, so I passed it to him for a layup. The way I figure it, I could have made the layup and made myself happy, but I was alaready happy about the steal and the chance to get two points for the team So I said, 'Why not give the ball to Lloyd, get myself an assist, and make two people happy?' That's what this game is all about and I think it is a major reason why Portland has been so successful." Twardzik's emphasis on the word "happy" was an accurate reflection of his basic attitude toward life: have a good time. Fudd is clearly the team's leading clown, keeping people loose with self-deprecating remarks and insults delivered toward various teammates. His humor is omnipresent.

Twardzik on his speed: "I've got a great first step, but after that there's a rapid decline. They measure football players at forty yards, but my best distance is ten feet." He shoots a shot that he calls the "springer"—which is his version of a jump shot except "that I can't jump enough to call it a jump shot." On Jack Ramsay's outlandish pants: "Pants? I thought his legs were tattooed." On constantly being labeled small: "I'm not a small guy. I'm on a campaign to stop being called little. I'm normal. In fact I tower over most people." On being informed at an autographing that two men had left a nearby bar just to get his autograph: "Boy, I must be a *real* drawing card." On being informed that his name had been inadvertently left off the All-Star balloting card: "Whatever write-in support I might get should inform the league office what kind of spellers are out there in the twenty-two cities." On why he passed up so many open jumpers: "I blame my two older brothers for that. We used to play on the playgrounds and whenever I took a jump shot, they'd call a time-out just to remind me they were the shooters in the family."

Maybe his brothers used to be the shooters in the family, but Dave has taken over the role now. In the championship season he compiled marks of .612 from the field—good enough to lead the league except that Fudd took one-half shot per game too few to qualify for the title, and shot an excellent .842 from the foul line. It is interesting to note that no player in NBA history—except Wilt Chamberlain—ever officially shot over .600 from the field for an entire season.

Still, according to Stu Inman, the Blazers' director of player personnel, Twardzik's shooting was really a bonus for the team, not a necessity. "Dave is probably a 50 percent shooter from 17 feet. But with Lionel Hollins and Maurice Lucas, plus Walton, putting the ball up pretty regularly we don't happen to need the perimeter shot from him. He is very clever at getting off shots underneath, and his judgment on the court is damn near impeccable. He's just one of those rare guys who just go into a game and make the other four guys play better." For Dave Twardzik the Trail Blazers were a "team of eleven working parts, all functional and all necessary in achieving our every game goal of winning. Statistics, all-star voting, and stuff like that are consolation prizes." It is, perhaps, the quality of his thinking that more than anything else makes Twardzik so valuable. "Dave's physical skills," said Inman, "are only adequate, but you add his brightness and tenacity and you have a very special basketball player. I rate him as high as anybody I've ever seen in terms of his mind actually being an asset in the course of a game. And most other players in that category, Walton, Bill Russell, Bill Bradley, Oscar, and a few others, had much more natural ability."

13

THE RESERVES

Lloyd Neal

*T*HAT LLOYD NEAL was one of the most courageous players in the NBA was made apparent to the basketball world when he participated in the 1977 playoffs while still unable to walk without limping noticeably. Neal's career, after three full injury-free seasons in which he missed a total of two games, and a fourth season marked by a few slight injuries that kept his games-played down to 68 (though his points per game average was a career-high 15.5), was dealt a cruel and painful blow with a serious knee injury which forced surgery during training camp in 1976. Neal's minutes played dropped from 2,320 the previous season to 955 in the championship season. Despite hard work the fragile knee was undependable the entire year and Neal registered career lows in all major statistical categories.

The 6'8" Neal, a native of Talbottom, Georgia, was a third-round draft choice out of Tennessee State in the 1972 draft. His powerful rebounding, deft shooting touch, and genial off-the-court personality soon endeared him to Portland fans, players, and management alike. Throughout the dismal early years of the Blazer franchise Neal performed with quiet distinction and intensity. As a center he averaged as many as 13.4 points per game and 10.5 rebounds (1972–73); the latter, representing a total of 967 rebounds, remains a Blazer all-time record. When Walton arrived, he moved over to power forward where he scored 12.3 and 15.5 points per game in two healthy seasons.

Larry Steele

The oldest player in point of service for the Blazers, as well as age, Larry Steele has been the archetypal reserve for most of his NBA career. In the championship season he averaged in double figures, for the first time in his career, 10.3 points per game, shooting .500 from the floor for the season. And he won a championship, a feeling which Steele says "took a while to sink in."

The last survivor from the Blazers' second year, Steele holds the somewhat dubious distinction of being the all-time Portland record holder for career fouls and career disqualifications. The marks, however, rather than being a negative sign, point up Larry Steele's greatest asset—aggressive defense. For six years he had been called upon, in Lenny Wilkins' words, "to harass the hell" out of whichever opposing forward or guard had a hot hand. The task is akin to a relief pitcher who always arrives with the bases full of people, a .300 hitter at bat, and a manager who says, "throw strikes." For six years Larry Steele had consistently "thrown strikes."

Steele felt that when the Blazers drafted him on the third round of the 1971 college draft (out of Kentucky) he received "the break of my life. Portland was a second-year team and I got a chance to improve my game as they improved. If I had been drafted by a more established team, I may not have had the chance to improve and certainly it would have been tougher to make the team."

A native of Breencastle, Indiana, Steele was a high school all-state player at nearby Brainbridge High. Recruited by the legendary Adoph Rupp, Steele chose Kentucky to play his college basketball, where he starred for three years as a sharp-shooting, hustling forward-guard. As a Blazer Steele did not begin to receive significant playing time during his rookie season until Stu Inman replaced Rolland Todd as coach. From bench sitter Steele went to starter, where he shot 50 percent from the field. Bob Wolf, in *Sporting News*, wrote that "all the young man needs is confidence. He came into the pros with a reputation as a great shooter but he has been reluctant to put it up." At the end of what had become a horrendous season Steele developed into a solid performer, one of the few bright spots in a difficult year. In 1973-74 under coach Jack McCloskey, Steele became a starter regularly for the first time. He ended up averaging a shade under ten points per game and continued to demonstrate his defensive capabilities. For the next two seasons Steele continued to start and continued to shoot brilliantly—.548 and .494 from the floor—though the Blazers as a team did not play with any kind of consistency. Then in the championship season Steele became a reserve under Jack Ramsay and produced the finest year of his career, averaging 10.3 points per game. Often characterized as an "overachiever," Larry Steele was the kind of overachiever that NBA coaches love to have on their teams.

JOHNNY DAVIS

During his first season in the NBA, 21-year-old guard Johnny Davis had seen only an average of 18 minutes

The Pride of Portland

playing time per game. Down the stretch, he had seen even less, and he didn't appear at all in Portland's opening round playoff victory over the Chicago Bulls. Yet, when Dave Twardzik was hurt in the fifth game of the Denver series, Davis stepped into a starting role, hit ten of 14 shots, scored 25 points, and led the Blazers to a victory over the Nuggets that advanced them to the Western Division finals. After Davis helped defeat the Lakers in four straight games, L.A. coach Jerry West said: "Davis is an outstanding young player with a great future in this league."

The reason Davis was able to step into the breech and perform so well was that, unlike so many young players, he was a team man all the way. To Davis, "basketball is not a one-on-one game. We're all eleven of us in it together. Even when I played in the playground I believed that the cats playing together were gonna win."

To Davis, who was born in Birmingham, Alabama, on October 21, 1955, taking responsibility came early. At age two, he moved to Detroit, settling in with his mother, his older brother, Lonnie, and his younger sister, Sharon, into the Brewster project, a rough-and-tumble outpost in the inner city. According to Davis, in Brewster, "nothing is taken for granted . . . not even your life."

From the time he started playing basketball at age 12, Davis took nothing for granted. As a senior at Detroit's Murray-Wright High School, Davis made several high school All-American teams, averaged 31 points a game, and received a grant-in-aid to Dayton University.

Even at that tender age, Davis had a superior attitude. "He kind of played the role with us his freshman year that he played with Portland last year," Dayton coach Don Donoher recalled. "He stepped in with a bunch of seniors his first year and we went all the way to the Western Regionals of the NCAA tournament before losing to UCLA in triple overtime.

"I remember UCLA tried to press us early in that game. Johnny broke their press on the dribble and went through the whole team. Bill Walton was back, and Johnny challenged him and laid it up off the glass right over the top of Walton. There was no more press after that."

Davis entered the NBA draft as a hardship case after his junior year. "I needed to help my family out financially," he said. Davis' mother underwent surgery in January of his junior year and was unable to resume her job. Said Davis, "She wanted me to get my degree, and she never asked me to go hardship. But there comes a point in a man's life when he has to make a decision."

Davis was Portland's second pick of the second round of the 1976 NBA draft. Said Jack Ramsay, "We drafted him for quickness, good defense, ability to penetrate. He surprised me in his ability to come into the game in a pressure situation. We didn't draft him with the thoughts of him starting. Except for a Jabbar or a Walton, you don't draft any college player and expect him to be a starter."

But Davis' willingness to learn and his hard work made him an important part of the championship team. When playing the off-guard, his speed made him impossible to press, and created many offensive opportunities for Hollins and the forwards. Bill Walton summed it up: "John was a big reason we won the championship. He came to play every night."

Corky Calhoun

Corky Calhoun, once described as the "backup man's backup man," was in so many ways almost the prototypical Portland Trail Blazer. He was first of all intelligent, then a team player, then an excellent defensive player. (His offensive weaknesses, particularly a reluctance to shoot, have severely limited his NBA playing time.) For the Blazers, Corky was, in the words of Jack Ramsay, a player "whose abilities suit our game very well."

Ramsay explained the signing of Calhoun one day before the 1976–77 season. "Stu Inman and I were both high on him. We needed an experienced pressure forward. Corky is a very good defensive player and ball handler and he's going to still develop into a good offensive player. We also can use him on some of the big guards around the league. He's excellent for us."

In discussing the Blazers, both starters and reserves, it has become almost cliché to repeat that each player was a devoted team player; for no one even wants to be labeled anything other than a team man. But in the case of the Blazers it was specifically accurate that the team that Stu Inman and Harry Glickman assembled was truly a "team" in the best senses of that word. Corky Calhoun, despite sporadic playing time and the disappointment that all players feel when such a situation confronts them, maintained a totally supportive, enthusiastic, and ready-to-play attitude. "I feel," said Corky, "I've been very lucky. With all the problems I've had, just look at what I've done. I've played in the NBA for six years. Millions of guys would like to do what I'm doing."

A native of Waukegan, Illinois, Calhoun attended college at the Ivy League's University of Pennsylvania, where he played under the University of Oregon's Dick Harter for three years, during which time his teams won 99 games and lost six. According to Joe Gilmartin in *Sporting News*, Calhoun was regarded by scouts as "intelligent, extremely unselfish, team oriented, fundamentally sound and very nice. In fact," added Gilmartin, "it's hard to get through a sentence on [Calhoun] without using the word 'nice.'"

A first-round draft choice of the Phoenix Suns, Calhoun no sooner had signed his contract before he donated money to his alma mater for a scholarship as a return for the scholarship he had received. That's exactly the sort of fellow Corky Calhoun is.

With Phoenix Calhoun averaged 6.0 and 8.2 points per game and in his third season was traded to Los Angeles, where he continued to see steady though reduced playing time. Despite a career field goal shooting percentage of approximately .460 and a highly respectable .762 from the foul line, Calhoun with the Lakers, as he had done with Phoenix, showed almost no desire to shoot. As a senior in college he averaged only 12.8 points per game, so zone-breaking jump shots thrown up from afar could never be expected from Corky, though one cannot help but wonder why he doesn't shoot—considering his statistical consistency—with a little more confidence and frequency.

Still it was defense for which he was primarily responsible on the Blazers. "Corky," said Stu Inman, "is a specialist in the best sense of that word. He can come off the bench to guard some of the toughest players in the league, like David Thompson or Julius Erving. He's a very intelligent player, who while he doesn't create shots, hits the open shot well. He fills a need for us."

HERM GILLIAM

It was the third quarter of the vital second game of the 1977 Western Division Championship Series, played at Los Angeles. After a tight first half of play, the Lakers had suddenly exploded to a nine-point lead and the Blazers were foundering. Lionel Hollins, who had kept Portland in the game in the first half, had cooled off; the Blazer front line was unable to get untracked. But Jack Ramsay once again made the perfect substitution, the one man on the team whose presence was so vital in those rare instances when the Blazers' offensive machine was clogged. He sent Herm Gilliam, the six-year veteran who was known to his teammates as "The Trickster."

Gilliam was a 6'3" guard who had starred at Purdue. He had been drafted by the Cincinnati Royals in 1969, then went to the expansion Buffalo Braves the next season. A trade brought him to the Atlanta Hawks in 1971, and during the next four years he averaged double figures. He played the 1975–76 season with Seattle.

The signing of Gilliam in the fall of 1976 was yet another shrewd move by Portland management, one that was a considerable risk for a team with the kind of passing game the Blazers liked to play. For Gilliam's forte was one-on-one basketball, the dazzling playground-style confrontations that, in Gilliam's case, meant a headlong drive to the basket culminated by one of his huge assortments of incredible shots that gave him his nickname.

Some observers argued that Gilliam, despite his talents, couldn't or wouldn't change his game after six years. But these observers were wrong. Said Jack Ramsay, Gilliam had to make "probably the most difficult adjustment of any player to the style of play we were using." But Gilliam, an intelligent, cooperative player, tried his very best. In fact, late in the season, the New Orleans Jazz approached Portland about a trade for Gilliam. Ramsay, knowing Gilliam would get more playing time in New Orleans, asked the veteran if he wanted the trade to go through. But Gilliam, after consulting with his wife, decided that he would rather fulfill his role on a team with a winning attitude than be traded.

Gilliam's role was as an offensive spark. At those rare times when the Blazers' offense had wound down to a crawl, Gilliam's theatrical display of basketball magic would provide a spark. And that second crucial game in Los Angeles was a perfect example. Immediately upon entering the game, Gilliam hit a bucket to stop the Los Angeles streak. Then, in the fourth quarter, with the score 91–84 Los Angeles, Gilliam went wild. He hit a 20-foot jumper, then three more baskets in succession to bring the Blazers within one. The lead changed hands twice, but L.A. still led with a minute left. Once again Gilliam took charge. He took a pass, faked, cut across the lane, then scooped the ball with his right hand over the outstretched fingertips of Kareem Abdul-Jabbar and into the bucket. It was the winning basket. "The Trickster" had come off the bench to score 24 magical points and spark the Blazers to a four-game sweep of the Lakers.

WALLY WALKER

Wally Walker was the Blazers' first choice in the 1976 NBA draft, the fifth choice overall. In four years at the University of Virginia, Walker had scored 1,849 points and shot .518 from the field. As a senior, he averaged 22.1 points per game, shot .548 from the field, and tore the tough Atlantic Coast Conference tournament apart with 73 points on .683 shooting in three games.

On the Blazers, Walker got little playing time. A small forward, he was third man behind starter Bob Gross and Larry Steele, who was enjoying a fine year. His talent was obvious, and his attitude fit well with the Blazers' team spirit. Said Ramsay at one point during the season, "If Walker were with a team that wasn't winning, he would be playing a lot more."

But when Walker had to play, he did the job. In the six games in which he had to play more than 20 minutes, he averaged 13.2 points and shot .507 from the field. More important, he played well in crucial spots in the playoffs, hitting 20 of 36 shots for a blistering .556. As an eleventh man, he did more than an eleventh man's job.

ROBIN JONES

Jack Ramsay's game plan for the 1976–77 season was built around defense, which was why the Trail Blazers signed Robin Jones on August 11, 1976. Jones was a 22-year-old native of St. Louis, Missouri, who had attended St. Louis University. A 6'9", 225-pound center, Jones was unable to find a spot in the NBA and went to Europe to play ball for the 1975–76 season.

Enthusiastic reports of his play in Europe attracted the attention of the Trail Blazers. Primarily, Jones was a defensive center who could be counted on to keep the opposing team from penetrating while Walton rested or suffered from foul trouble. Jones was a fine fundamental rebounder, but was not an offensive threat.

While Walton was healthy, Jones patiently waited on the bench. But during Walton's absence from the lineup due to injuries, Jones proved a valuable member of the Blazers. Eight times he led the team in rebounding, pulling down an impressive 16 boards against Cleveland and 15 against the rugged front line of the Washington Bullets.

THREE

THE FALL FROM THE THRONE

14

THE 1977–78 SEASON

Capturing the NBA crown in modern basketball is the pinnacle of professional sports success. In the early days of the NBA, dynasties dominated the league for years. Minneapolis had won six NBA championships; the Celtics an astounding 13. But in the last ten years, with expansion, the rigors of the travel and crowded schedule, free agentry, the abundance of good players and coaches, had made the development of a dynasty a thing of the past.

The ambition of the Portland franchise, despite the above, was to develop a team that would prove itself year after year. And prove itself it did in 1978 and 1979. But the proving was done not with repeat NBA championships, but through survival of injuries and controversy that would have sunk a less stable franchise. As described below, the Blazers were perhaps the strongest franchise in league history before the storm struck; the reaction of the management, players, and fans to the tremendous difficulties demonstrates vividly how firmly entrenched was the pride of Portland.

For the first time in their history, the Portland management was not faced with the prospect of rebuilding in preparation for the next season. Instead, they had a high performance basketball machine that just needed some fine tuning to smooth over some minor rough spots.

Two changes in the Portland roster for the 1977–78 season were determined by the Blazers' primary goal for the new year: better defense. Portland had finished first in the Pacific Division and third in the NBA in offense (111.7 per game), but only fourth in the division in defense (allowing 106.2 per game). When the Blazers played at home, the enthusiasm of the fans often triggered the devastating fast-break offense that blew opposing teams off the court. On the road, however, tenacious defense was absolutely necessary to keep the visiting team in the game. For this reason, Portland concentrated on better defense to boost the team's 14–27 road mark of 1976–77.

One Portland defensive weakness was made strikingly apparent during the finals against Philadelphia. In several games, 6'6" Doug Collins had given the Blazers fits. When Lionel Hollins got into foul trouble or sat down for a rest, the Blazers had no guard with the size and quickness to match up against the versatile 76er. Defense against big, quick guards like Collins, David Thompson, and George Gervin was the reason T. R. Dunn, a 6'4" rookie from Alabama, the Blazers' third draft choice, replaced Herm Gilliam on the Portland roster.

A vote by the NBA owners to reduce the roster from 12 to 11 men necessitated another decision that was finally made with defense in mind. Wally Walker and Corky Calhoun were the competitors for the final spot on the roster. Both had seen limited time during the regular season. Walker had the scoring edge, but Calhoun was a skilled defender who had played a small but critical role in several playoff situations. The likable Calhoun made the squad, and Walker ended up on the Seattle Supersonics.

The Pride of Portland

The third roster change for 1977–78 resulted from the need for a stronger replacement for Bill Walton. Robin Jones had done an adequate job defensively, but the Blazer offense shut down with him in the game. Portland went out looking for a more offensive-minded reserve center who would keep the offense rolling, provide adequate defense and rebounding, and who could fill in at forward against teams with very tall front lines.

The solution to the problem was trading Robin Jones to Houston for Tom Owens, an intelligent six-year veteran who had once averaged 15.1 points per game.

In sharp contrast to the preceding seasons, basketball analysts unanimously picked the Portland Trail Blazers to finish first in the Pacific Division. But once again, the Pacific Division was by far the strongest in the league, even stronger than the preceding year, and the competition would be keen.

Portland's dominance in this strong division depended on two things. The first was the avoidance of key injuries, especially injuries to Bill Walton. Increased poise and maturity, together with the addition of Tom Owens, would make Portland a better team without Walton. But few observers thought a Blazer squad without the big redhead was of championship quality.

The second requirement was better consistency, especially on the road. Portland's previous season and playoffs had been marked by stretches of brilliance, 40-point-plus quarters that rocked the opposition. But Jack Ramsay was aiming for not 20 or 30 but 48 minutes of perfect basketball.

In the first 60 games of the 1977–78 season, Ramsay got closer to that goal than anyone dreamed possible. In the first 120 days of this campaign, Portland roared to an astounding 50–10 mark that perched them on top of their division by 12½ games, and on top of the entire league by nine. Said Milwaukee Buck coach Don Nelson, the Blazers had become "a team for all time."

The season had opened October 21 in Seattle, and the Blazers began with an auspicious 106–99 win. Bill Walton had returned to action after injuring his back chopping wood during the preseason, and his 18 points and 13 rebounds sparked Portland.

The Blazers returned home to face San Antonio on Sunday, October 23. Before their fifteenth consecutive sellout crowd, the Portland players received their championship rings from Commissioner Larry O'Brian. Then they proceeded to blast the Spurs, as they roared from a 90–88 deficit to a 122–102 lead.

The Blazers trounced Buffalo at home and dropped a tough 111–108 game at Denver, before returning to Memorial Coliseum for a nationally televised game with the Philadelphia 76ers. In a hard-fought rematch of playoff foes, the Blazers rallied from behind to take out a 98–94 win.

With that challenge past, Portland really began to roll. They followed with four more consecutive home victories to make their mark 8–1, split four games on the road, then returned home for four more wins to go 14–3.

With Maurice Lucas hurt, the Blazers traveled to Los Angeles. But Lloyd Neal responded to the challenge by hitting 15 of 19 from the floor and three of three from the foul line for a career-high 33 points to lead his team to a 100–93 victory.

That road win against Los Angeles marked a stretch in which Portland won seven of nine games away from home. The traveling problems that at times had plagued the young squad of the previous season were finally vanquished.

By the all-star break in early February, the Blazers' dominance of the NBA was clearly established. Portland

The Pride of Portland

was 40–8, nine games ahead in their division. They were a perfect 26–0 at home (44 consecutive wins over two seasons), and a sparkling 14–8 on the road. In the last five games before the break, Portland had won by consecutive margins of 23, 35, 35, 20, and 20 points.

The game Portland was playing was team basketball at its best. The Blazers led the league in defense with 100.4 per game, an incredible 5.7 point drop from their record of a year before. Although without a single scorer in the top twenty in the league, they led in victory margin (10.1), by five points. During the first 48 games, nine different players had led the team in scoring, seven in assists and five in rebounding. The Blazers had won all six games Lucas had missed and both games center Bill Walton didn't play.

NBA players and coaches alike regarded the Blazers with something akin to awe. Rick Barry told *Sports Illustrated*, "This team deserves any comparison anybody wants to make. The old Celtics, the Knicks, Philly with Wilt, L.A. with Wilt, anybody. It's a clinic whenever you play them. They get the ball out and ram it down your throat. Walton is a great center who does everything, and all the rest complement each other. The Blazers may be the most ideal team ever put together."

On January 31 Don Nelson had seen his Milwaukee team put together an almost perfect first half against the Blazers. The Bucks scored 39 points in the first quarter, shot 60 percent for the half—only to find themselves trailing by two points! Portland went on to win 136–116, and Nelson commented to *SI*, "Ninety percent of what they do is automatic, everyone picks it up. The Celtics had role-playing, defensive and offensive specialists. Here the attack is more general. Everybody on the Blazers can beat you at either end."

Jack Ramsay summed it up: "Now we are more poised. We concentrate better. We have fewer dry spells on offense, fewer lapses on defense." That was exactly what Ramsay had aimed for at the beginning of the season.

After a five-day rest at the all-star break, the Blazers got even hotter. For the first time in 41 games, Walton failed to score in double figures, but Portland bested Cleveland 94–88 in Cleveland, then added another road win at Indiana. On Sunday, February 12, David Thompson hit a jump shot with 19 seconds left, as the Denver Nuggets ended Portland's home victory streak at 44 games. This game was decided by two points, 103–101, despite the fact that Maurice Lucas was held to eight, and Lionel Hollins had connected on only six of 22 shots from the floor.

A new streak started as three home victories sandwiched a road loss, again to the Nuggets. Then the Blazers hacked out four consecutive road victories.

On February 28 the Blazers returned home to face Philadelphia. A win over the 76ers would give Portland a 50–10 record after 60 games. This .833 clip would, if extended for the rest of the season, have given the Blazers 68 wins. Only the 1971–72 Los Angeles Lakers had managed more (69), and the mark would tie the next two best teams, the 1966–67 Philadelphia 76ers and 1972–73 Celtics. Portland's road record of 20–9 was a better win percentage (.690) than any other NBA team's overall record. The fiftieth victory would clinch a playoff berth 22 games before the season's end.

The Blazers did beat the 76ers that day. But once again a Philadelphia game signaled a change in the fortune of Portland. A 146–104 rout of the Sixers at the beginning of the 1976–77 season marked Portland's arrival as a contender. The four wins and two losses in the final round of the playoffs gave the Blazers the NBA crown and established them as a premier team in the league. Now, a Philadelphia game was a double-edged mark—on the positive side, the statistical high point of the Blazers' almost magical season; on the negative side, this game began a period of incredible reverses that would cast serious doubts not only on the Blazers' ability to defend their crown but, eventually, on their integrity as a franchise as well.

An unusual number of injuries had bothered the Blazers all year. Lucas had missed a number of games with leg ailments. Twardzik had ankle problems, then a virus that took him out of some games and limited his effectiveness when he returned. Key reserve Lloyd Neal, who had responded magnificently in 12 starting assignments, experienced recurring knee problems, and Larry Steele was hampered by bad feet.

Portland had continued to win, because the loss of one man could be overcome. But beginning with this Philadelphia game, the Blazers were to experience an avalanche of injuries. With eight minutes left in the first half, Bill Walton, who had missed only two of 60 games, sprained his left ankle. Walton had already been hobbled by problems in the ball area of his right foot, and overcompensating had weakened his left. Although no one knew it at the time, when Walton left the floor of Memorial Coliseum that day, he left the Blazer lineup for the rest of the season. On March 5 team doctor Bob Look operated on Walton's right foot, removing four nerve stems between the second and third toes.

The next night Portland made up a previously snowed-out game at Madison Square Garden. Lloyd Neal, still starting in place of the recently returned Lucas, collided with Maurice in the first quarter and reinjured his knee. Neal, a vital reserve with Walton out, was himself to miss the rest of the regular season. Despite Tom Owen's 25 points, the Knicks beat the Blazers for the first time all season.

Despite those two injuries, the homecourt magic still worked as the Blazers returned to Memorial Coliseum for wins over Cleveland and Milwaukee. But then started a disastrous four-game road trip that began with an anemic offensive showing in an 84–82 loss to New Orleans, followed by a loss to lowly Houston. At Atlanta, the Blazers not only lost the game, they lost Maurice Lucas for six games with a strained tendon in his left leg. A fourth consecutive loss at Buffalo finished the trip.

Now missing three big men—Walton, Lucas, and Neal—Portland returned home to lose its first two games before a victory over Atlanta. The next night, in a courageous performance, Portland bested Seattle 102–96 to clinch the best record in the Western Conference. Lionel Hollins and Owens had 26 each. For a day, the two consecutive wins made prospects seem brighter.

But once again the hammer fell. On March 23, in Milwaukee, Bob Gross, who had played the previous game with a pain-killer injected into his left ankle, suffered a stress fracture of that joint. Larry Steele also went out of the game with tendonitis in his knees. Portland was down to just seven men.

The Blazers had already picked up six-year NBA veteran Willie Norwood to replace Neal. Now they hurriedly added 6'10" center Dale Schleuter, a ten-year veteran who had played for the Blazers in the 1970–71 and 1971–72 seasons; and Jackie Dorsey, a 6'7" forward from Georgia who had played seven games for Denver before being released.

Schleuter got to Cobo Arena in Detroit 15 minutes before game time, boosting the Portland roster up to the NBA minimum of eight players, but the Pistons easily beat the Blazers. With a starting lineup of Willie Norwood, Corky Calhoun, Tom Owens, Johnny Davis, and Lionel Hollins, Portland fell to Philadelphia 116–110, giving the Blazers a slim two and a half game edge in the race for the

The Pride of Portland

best record in the NBA. When the teams had met just one month earlier, the Blazer lead had been nine games.

Lucas returned to the lineup, but he was hampered by yet another physical problem—sore wrists. In their next six games the Blazers eked out only a dramatic 103–101 win at Los Angeles.

With two games remaining, Portland needed only one win to give them the best record in the NBA, $50,000, and homecourt advantage should they meet the 76ers in the playoffs. As they had done so many times in the preceding two seasons, they met the crucial challenge in the first game, against the Denver Nuggets, who had spoiled their 44 home game win streak earlier in the year. Maurice Lucas fought off his pain to score 31 points and haul down

FINAL NBA STANDINGS 1977–78

EASTERN CONFERENCE

Atlantic Division

* Philadelphia	55	27	.671	—
* New York	43	39	.524	12
Boston	32	50	.390	23
Buffalo	27	55	.329	28
New Jersey	24	58	.293	31

Central Division

* San Antonio	52	30	.634	—
* Washington	44	38	.537	8
* Cleveland	43	39	.524	9
* Atlanta	41	41	.500	11
New Orleans	39	43	.476	13
Houston	28	54	.341	24

WESTERN CONFERENCE

Midwest Division

* Denver	48	34	.585	—
* Milwaukee	44	38	.537	4
Chicago	40	42	.488	8
Detroit	38	44	.463	10
Kansas City	31	51	.373	17
Indiana	31	51	.373	17

Pacific Division

* Portland	58	24	.707	—
* Phoenix	49	33	.598	9
* Seattle	47	35	.572	11
* Los Angeles	45	37	.549	13
Golden State	43	39	.524	15

* Playoff teams

19 rebounds. Larry Steele, who had returned to action the game before, contributed 14, and Tom Owens had 13 rebounds. Buoyed by this big win, the Blazers rolled over Los Angeles before their forty-first consecutive sellout crowd (an NBA record). A victory over the Lakers had sent the Blazers into the 1977 playoffs; now the team hoped this triumph would mean equally good fortune for 1978.

15

THE 1978 PLAYOFFS

*I*N 1977 the unproven Trail Blazers had to survive a rugged best-of-three series to advance to the second round. This year, their Pacific Division championship gave them nine precious days in which to further rest their wounded.

Portland's 58–24 record was three games better than the Philadelphia 76ers, who had enjoyed far better health throughout the year. The Blazers had finished nine games ahead of a Pacific Division so strong that the last-place team, Golden State, finished four games above .500. Portland led the NBA in defense, an achievement made even more remarkable by the fact that the Blazers' defensive statistics were not aided by a ball control offense. Portland's tenacious checking held their opponents shooting percentage to .449, and the average Blazer margin of victory, 6.2 points, was the highest in the league by over a point.

Winning while physically under par in a grueling seven-game playoff series was, of course, a different matter. Gross was lost for the playoffs. Walton and Neal were practicing, but not yet anywhere near peak form. No observer, however, ventured to write off a Portland team whose courage and discipline had been proven so many times before.

Seattle bested Los Angeles in three games, and once again, ironically, Portland had the hottest team in basketball as their first opponent. Under coach Bob Hopkins, the Sonics got off to a dismal 5–17 start. Lenny Wilkins, a former Blazer and Sonic coach, replaced Hopkins, and Seattle coasted to 42 victories in their last 60 games to finish third in the Pacific Division, two games behind the second-place Phoenix Suns.

Wilkins had installed an entirely new starting lineup for Seattle. Hopkins had opened the season with Mike Green at center, Bruce Seals and Paul Silas at forwards, and Slick Watts and Fred Brown at guard. Wilkins dealt away Watts and Green, and designated Silas and Brown as super-subs. As a starting lineup he offered Marvin Webster at center, John Johnson and Jack Sikma at forward, and Dennis Johnson and Gus Williams at guard.

Immediately, the new configuration clicked. Most of the Sonic firepower came from the guard triumvirate. Speedy Gus Williams led the team in scoring with 18.1 points per game and dished out 294 assists. Dennis Johnson, a 6'4" second-year man out of Pepperdine, was a ferocious defender and shot blocker who was capable of some big offensive games. Fred Brown came off the bench to average 16.6 points, shooting .488 from "downtown."

Marvin Webster was a smooth passer in the pivot, and John Johnson and Jack Sikma were competent short-range shooters. But the front line's biggest strength was offensive rebounding. Seattle led the NBA in that category. Webster, Sikma, and 13-year veteran Paul Silas alone pulled down 846 offensive boards, nearly 400 more than the Blazer front line. Dennis Johnson led the league's guards with 156 rebounds at the offensive end of the court.

The Pride of Portland

Strong offensive rebounding slowed down opponents' fast breaks, which contributed to the Sonics' finishing second to Portland in team defense. Webster was an excellent shot blocker, which discouraged penetration, and the quickness of the guards was a major disruptive force.

To beat Seattle, Jack Ramsay knew the Blazers, first of all, had to stop the guards, who had outscored the L. A. backcourt 154–89 in the opening round. Secondly, they had to keep Silas, Sikma, and Webster away from the offensive board. Portland shot .483 (a team record) for the year, while the Sonics shot a poor .447. Without the benefit of second and third shots, the Sonics could be outdueled from the floor.

With a healthy Gross, Lucas, and Walton, the Blazer front line had been able to take advantage of the less experienced Sonics in winning three of four regular season games. In the playoffs, Ramsay hoped Steele could play Johnson even and the injured Walton could neutralize Webster. Lucas' ability to dominate the rookie Sikma could well be the key to close games.

The Portland scenario worked to perfection in the first quarter of Game One, played in Memorial Coliseum in Portland on Wednesday night, April 19. The Blazers ran to a 34–23 lead in front of the roaring capacity crowd. Portland outrebounded the Sonics 18–7 in that stanza, with Maurice Lucas pulling down nine rebounds.

In the second quarter, Wally Walker and Fred Brown came off the bench to score eight points apiece to keep Seattle in the game. Walton came back from his 22-game layoff to hit his first five shots and snare eight rebounds. Larry Steele completely outclassed John Johnson, hitting six of nine from the floor and five of five from the line for 17 big first-half points. The Blazers led at intermission, 53–46.

Even in the midst of this prosperity, however, there was

a telltale sign of trouble. Walton was playing with great courage, but the Seattle front line noticed he was limping. Said Marvin Webster after the game, "He was nowhere near 100 percent, 'bout 70 percent I'd say. Me and Jack were going to take it to him."

In the second half, Seattle did take it to the Portland front line. Walton, hobbling, was unable to get down the floor quickly on offense, and the Blazers started popping away from the perimeter instead of running their offense. Steele, after his great first half, missed all six shots in the second half. After the first quarter, Lucas only managed two more rebounds for the rest of the game and shot a miserable 3–15. Perhaps the most telling statistic is that Walton, the best passing center in basketball and the heart of the Blazer offense, had only two assists in the entire game.

Only Johnny Davis kept Portland in front through most of the third quarter. After the guard from Dayton hit two free throws with 2:14 left to give Portland a 75–72 edge, Marvin Webster hit a fadeaway jumper and Fred Brown pumped in five straight points to put Seattle up 79–75.

Portland, after falling behind by 12, scraped to within five with 2:16 left, on four courageous points by an exhausted Walton. But Dennis Johnson soared high in the air to block a Hollins jumper, drove down the court for a solo basket, and Seattle went on to win 104–95. The homecourt advantage that the Blazers had worked so long to get was gone.

The Seattle front court domination in the second half had been the fatal blow. Sikma had seven rebounds and 12 points in the second half, totally outplaying Maurice Lucas. Webster hit for a game-high 24, and the Seattle guards outscored Portland's 52–39.

Seattle continued to roll in the first half of Game Two, played again in Portland on Friday night, April 21. Bill

The Pride of Portland

Walton, playing in obvious pain, scored ten points and pulled down six rebounds, but Gus Williams led the Sonics to a 49-40 halftime lead.

The Blazers, their backs already against the wall, came out to open the second half without Bill Walton, whose left foot pained him too much to play. Perhaps inspired by Walton's courage in the first half, Portland came out red hot, scoring the first nine points to tie the game at 49. Johnny Davis, embarrassed by Williams in the first half, threw in 13 in the third quarter as the lead seesawed back and forth.

The score was tied with 1:46 left in the game. Maurice Lucas, who had turned the tables in this game, intimidating Sikma and sweeping the boards, banked in a jumper to give the Blazers a 95-93 lead with 1:17 left. Lucas then forced a jump ball, won the tap, but Hollins was called for an offensive foul, his sixth. Corky Calhoun then stepped into the hero's circle, rebounding a Webster miss, hitting the first of two foul shots a few seconds later, then grabbing the miss of his second shot to ice the game. The series was tied at one game apiece.

The joy of this tremendous team effort was short-lived, however. The next day, Portland announced that Bill Walton had broken a bone in his left foot and would miss the rest of the playoffs. Lloyd Neal, barely able to walk, was joining Gross and Walton on the sidelines.

The crippled Blazers couldn't regroup in time for Game Three in Seattle's Memorial Coliseum on Sunday, April 23. The Sonics tried to hand the game to the Blazers, shooting a horrendous 22 percent in the first half. But Portland couldn't keep the Sonics from snaring 17 offensive rebounds, and Seattle managed a one-point halftime lead.

The game became a rout in the second half when John Johnson hit nine of 12 to get the Seattle offense untracked. For the game Seattle outrebounded Portland 71-40, as

Webster hauled down 23 and Sikma 12. The final score was Seattle 99, Portland 84.

TV scheduling gave the Blazers three much needed days off before Game Four, to be played Thursday night, April 27, in Seattle. Ramsay and his squad used this time well, managing what Bob Robinson of *The Oregonian* called "one of the most magnificent efforts in the Blazers' eight-year history."

The front line, led by an inspired Maurice Lucas, turned the 71–40 rebounding deficit to a 37–35 Portland advantage. Johnny Davis harassed Gus Williams and Fred Brown. And most of all, Lionel Hollins contributed perhaps the best game of his career, scoring 35 points on 15–28 from the floor and five of six from the line.

After an even first period, the Blazers surged in a blistering second quarter. Corky Calhoun led the rush with 11 of his 16 points coming in that stanza, as Portland took a 57–45 halftime lead.

Portland scuffled to stay in front as Hollins poured in bucket after bucket. But as the game came down to the wire, Seattle found a hero of its own—6'11" Jack Sikma. With 4:02 left, Sikma's two free throws brought Seattle within one. After a Portland basket, Sikma hit a layup, Silas tied the score with a charity toss, then the rookie from Illinois Wesleyan contributed a three-point play. With 2:23 left, it was a 96–95 lead for Seattle.

The two hot hands for Portland, Hollins and Sikma, traded jumpers, then Corky Calhoun made one of two from the line. The score was deadlocked at 98 with 29 seconds left.

Seattle brought the ball up court, working for a good shot. With four seconds left on the time clock, Sikma squeezed open on the baseline and whirled around for a jumper. Seattle 100–98.

The game wasn't over. Hollins had two chances to send

The Pride of Portland

the game into overtime, the second a six-foot baseline jumper which bounced off the rim as the buzzer sounded. Despite their incredible effort, Portland had come up two points short, and was down three games to one.

An emotional Jack Ramsay summed it up: "There's not a great deal you can say about a game like that. Our people played to their maximum. We just didn't quite have enough to hold them off."

With awesome odds against them, Portland rallied for one last effort. Syndicated basketball columnist Peter Vecsey writing in the New York *Post* said it all: "The Blazers do not intend to shrivel up and die just because the team has suffered crucial casualties.... They may be physically inferior to the perfectly healthy Sonics, but they have proved they are far superior emotionally and mentally."

In Portland's Game Five 113–89 blowout of Seattle, no Blazer better demonstrated his intelligence and commitment than center Tom Owens. Jack Ramsay said that he didn't "know if anyone has worked harder to get into what we do than Tom Owens. He's extremely bright and has a great retention for basketball matters."

Owens couldn't trigger the fast break like Walton, but when the Blazers set up their pattern offense, he was superb. In Game Five, he hit 12 of 17 from the floor and seven for ten from the line for 31 points. He dished out six assists, set perfect picks, and held Marvin Webster to just eight rebounds.

Maurice Lucas chipped in 24 points and 13 rebounds, as Portland outshot Seattle 53 percent to 47 percent, outassisted them 24–14, and outrebounded them 40–38. The game was a glorious going-away present for the faithful Portland crowd.

But a heart cannot indefinitely sustain a critically injured body, and Seattle finally turned out the lights on the 1977–78 season with a 105–94 victory on their homecourt.

The Pride of Portland

Exceptional performances by Maurice Lucas and Johnny Davis, in what would be his final game as a Blazer, couldn't stand up to a great team game by the physically stronger Super Sonics.

After the Western Conference Championship series of 1977, when the Blazers swept the Los Angeles Lakers in four games, Maurice Lucas had graciously said of Kareem Abdul-Jabbar, "He's the most respected player in the league because he never bows his head. Such great inner strength! You may beat his team, but you never beat him."

That kind of inner strength had been demonstrated even more vividly by the Trail Blazers of 1978. The Blazers weren't defeated or beaten—they simply lost four basketball games. They took the setback with typical poise and class, making no excuses and generously praising their opponents.

Jack Ramsay commented to *The Oregonian* on what this game meant to him. "I'm proud of this team. I don't know that I've ever been prouder of a team, even last year's club."

Maurice Lucas added: "We made some mistakes and we paid for them. But we played with a lot of guts. When you play with all your heart the way we did, that's all you can do."

In typical fashion, Portland fans knew their team had done all it could do. Fifteen hundred fans greeted the team on its return from Seattle, chanting, "We're still number one" and "We love you, Blazers."

16

THE 1978–79 SEASON:
Controversy and Challenge

AT THE END OF THE 1978 SEASON Portland fans had been buoyed by the courageous performance of the team in the playoffs, by an extraordinarily fine collegiate draft enjoyed by the Blazers, and by the prospect of having a healthy team, especially a healthy Bill Walton, for 1979. That hope was shattered on August 4, 1978, when Jack Scott read a statement to the press and public in which Walton demanded to be traded. Central to the demand were allegations that the Portland franchise had, in its treatment of Walton and other players, violated ethical medical practices, jeopardizing the health and well-being of the athletes.

Walton's problems had their roots in the injury to his left foot that he had suffered on February 28 of the past year. Examination showed that a nerve problem in the ball area of his right foot had led him to overcompensate and weaken the left foot. On March 5 Dr. Bob Cook had operated to correct the nerve problem in the right foot.

The right foot came around, but the left foot continued to be a problem. On March 28, despite the administration of what the Blazers called "oral medication"—either Butazolidin or Decadron—Walton found he was still unable to play. He didn't suit up for the rest of the season.

Despite having practiced very little, Walton played 34 minutes in Portland's first playoff game with Seattle. After the game, he could not walk without pain. When he still could not run by the next game, Dr. Cook determined that Walton could take an injection of a local anesthetic, Xylocaine, if he wanted to.

The prospects of the administration of a local anesthetic disturbed Walton in light of what had happened to his teammate Bob Gross earlier in the season. In early March, Gross's ankle had begun to bother him. Cook diagnosed the problem as tendonitis. No X ray was taken. By March 18 the pain in his ankle was so severe that he needed an injection of Xylocaine to play against Atlanta. Although Cook later said, "Almost without exception we get an X ray before medication is given," Gross still had not been X rayed. Three nights later, against Seattle, Gross needed three injections. By the time the Blazers reached Milwaukee, the pain was so great they had to inject a longer-lasting anesthetic. The doctor had to shoot three times before he found the right spot that deadened the pain. Gross, his foot totally numb, went out to play. He fractured his foot. "I didn't feel anything when the bone fractured," Gross said. "I only heard the noise." While the question of whether the treatment of Gross was unethical was uncertain, the fact that it was ill-advised was unquestionable.

Walton weighed what happened to Gross, but he knew the championship depended on his participation. Besides, Cook was his friend. He took the injection and played. But even with that, after 15 minutes of playing time in the first half, he had to sit out the game.

X rays taken after the game showed no fracture. But the pain became more intense, and further pictures were taken. Saturday morning, the fracture was found—a broken tarsal navicular bone below the left ankle.

After the season was over, Walton began to have doubts about the wisdom of his having been persuaded to play on his hurt foot. Rumors swirled that the Blazers had been in possession of X rays showing the fracture before the game in which he had taken the pain-killer, although these rumors were vigorously denied by the team. By late July Walton had decided he could not play for the Blazers again. On August 1 Walton and his advisers—Jack Scott and attorney John Bassett—met with Portland management in the O'Hare Hilton in Chicago. In that meeting, the Trail Blazers agreed to Walton's demand to be traded; both sides agreed to keep a low public profile during the controversy that was sure to ensue.

On August 4 Jack Scott read a statement of Walton's that said, in part: "This was the most difficult decision I've ever had to make concerning my basketball career. The tremendous loyalty and support of my teammates and Trail Blazer fans have made my decision that much tougher. Never in my life as an athlete have I seen a more dedicated and sincere group of sports fans as those who support the Blazers.

"My biggest loss is my teammates, our fans and having to leave an area and people that my family and I have come to love. I only hope that when I return as an opponent and visitor, the Trail Blazer boosters will treat me with the same love as they always have."

In keeping with his agreement, Walton would not comment on the situation further. But both Scott and Bassett did. Giving fuel to the controversial claim of X rays showing the fracture before the pain-killer was administered, Scott said, "If he [Walton] had any doubts about the wisdom of his decision, after seeing those X rays they were eliminated." Bassett threatened legal action if the Blazers didn't go through with a trade, claiming that the Blazers' medical treatment violated provisions of Walton's contract. Because of the comments of Scott and Bassett, many observers publicly speculated that Scott and Bassett had prodded Walton to reach the decision to leave, possibly in order to get the substantial commissions that would accrue after Walton signed a huge new contract elsewhere.

The Blazer management made a simple public statement, issued by Glickman: "Our president Larry Weinberg and I are absolutely shocked by Walton's decision. There was nothing in any prior conversation that he had with anyone in our organization to suggest that he was unhappy or that he was going to ask for a trade." Privately, the Blazer management examined its behavior in the situation. While there was no doubt, as with all medical treatment, hindsight revealed wiser courses of action in certain circumstances. But the Blazer management found no serious wrongdoing, and to their credit no scapegoat was thrown to the public.

For weeks, rumors of trades flew as Walton met with other teams. But as the season approached it became clear that it was unlikely Walton would be ready to play until very late in the season. No team was willing to give up important players for an athlete who might not be able to play for an entire year. No trade was made, and perhaps because Walton was unwilling to go through with the threats made by Scott and Bassett, he dropped them as his agents, eventually using the services of a UCLA alumnus. After conflicting statements about eventually returning to Portland, Walton finally signed a $1 million a year contract with San Diego in the spring of 1979. For Portland, the magnificent but all too brief era of Bill Walton was at an end.

By the time training camp got under way for the 1979

The Pride of Portland

season, the Walton furor had quieted. But the Blazers were unfortunately confronted with a rash of injury problems that made the end of 1978 look rosy. Gross had not yet recovered from the stress fracture and would be unable to open the season. Lionel Hollins was slow recovering from knee surgery. Dave Twardzik had kidney problems, and Lucas had problems with his right hand that on October 11 was diagnosed as a fracture of a spur around the joint of a finger. In their last exhibition game, the Blazers had available only Tom Owens, T. R. Dunn, and seven rookies.

Fortunately, that rookie crop was one of the finest in the NBA in years. The Trail Blazers had shrewdly worked to obtain three first-round and two second-round picks for the 1978 college draft. The Moses Malone trade gave Portland the option of taking Buffalo's number one pick in either 1978 or 1979. When the Braves' record indicated they would have the third overall pick, Portland decided to exercise its option for 1978.

The priority for that pick was obviously frontline help. With Walton's clouded future, with the likelihood of retirement of Lloyd Neal, the Blazers needed a player who could play both strong forward and center. When Glickman, Inman, and Ramsay examined the 1978 collegiate crop, they were delighted to find a player who had the ability and the attitude to become a future star in the Portland system—Mychal Thompson from The University of Minnesota. To ensure their ability to select Thompson, The Blazers traded their number three pick for Indiana's number one pick, reluctantly parting with guard Johnny Davis in the process.

But Thompson, perhaps the best big man in the draft since Walton, seemed worth the price. A consummate team player, Thompson in three years had averaged 23.4 points per game, 10.7 rebounds, shot .574 from the field, and led the Big Ten Conference centers in assists. His superb outlet passing triggered a blistering Minnesota fast break. An indication of his relative talent was a game in his junior year in which he destroyed Indiana's Kent Benson, scoring 35 points against the player who was the first pick in the 1977 college draft.

The Blazers' second pick in the first round (from Seattle via Detroit) was the seventh overall. With Johnny Davis gone, the priority was a quality guard, and Portland took an ideal player—Ron Brewer of the University of Arkansas.

Brewer was an extraordinary leaper and shooter who had led Arkansas into the 1978 NCAA Championship Game against Kentucky. He was a superb passer, and his hands, trained for quickness by years of playing on bumpy courts in his native Fort Smith, Arkansas, produced many steals. He had a great competitive attitude, and with all the shooting talent on the Arkansas team, Brewer had been the man who wanted and got the ball in clutch situations.

Satisfied with their first two picks, Portland traded its third 1978 first-round selection to the Golden State Warriors in exchange for the Warriors' 1980 or 1981 first-round picks. On the second round, their second selection was a rugged 6'10" center from Florida A&M named Cleamon Johnson, a hardworking big man with great timing and shot-blocking ability.

Despite the encouraging performance of the rookies, Portland's prospects as the year opened were less than promising. Lucas and Gross were on the disabled list, and Hollins and Twardzik were sub-par. The tone of the first part of the season was set in the opener on October 15, played before the usual sellout crowd of 12,666. The Chicago Bulls beat the Blazers 108 to 97, the first time the Bulls had beaten Portland at home in five years. The con-

The Pride of Portland

trast to the year before, when Portland had opened with 26 consecutive home victories, was stunning.

The Blazers came back to beat Kansas City two nights later, with rookie Thompson tossing in 37. But both Twardzik and Hollins were hurt in that game. By October 24 the Blazers' record was 1–4, and they were down to the league-minimum eight men. However, once again, Ramsay rallied his beleaguered troops. With Thompson scoring 29 and Owens 24, the Blazers scored an incredible 104–102 victory over the defending NBA champion Washington Bullets. This triumph indicated that although the Blazers were not likely to be the 1979 NBA champions, they would certainly be in a battle for a playoff spot and would have a lot to say about who would be the eventual winner.

It wasn't until March that the Blazers really began to get rolling. Then, with Ramsay playing a big front line of Thompson, Lucas, and Owens, and with guard Ron Brewer having become accustomed to the Portland system, the Blazers ripped off eight victories in nine games to surge past San Diego and clinch a playoff spot.

Despite the fact that Lucas had missed 13 games, Hollins 18, Twardzik 18, and Gross 29, Portland finished eight games above .500, finishing only seven games behind the Pacific Division leading Seattle Supersonics. Despite numerous problems, Lucas had averaged 20.4 points per game. Owens had a magnificent year, finishing ninth in the league in field goal percentage (.548) enroute to an 18.4 average. Despite missing 18 games and being still bothered by the knee on which he had been operated, Lionel Hollins averaged 15.4 points per game and dished out 325 assists. Both first-round draft choices had been very impressive; Thompson averaged 14.7 points per game, grabbed 604 rebounds, and led the team with 134 blocked shots. Brewer, third on the team with 2,454 minutes played, averaged 13.3 points per game and had 102 steals. Both Thompson and Brewer were named to the NBA All-Rookie Team.

FINAL NBA STANDINGS 1978–79

EASTERN CONFERENCE

Atlantic Division

* Washington	54	28	.659	—
* Philadelphia	47	35	.573	7
* New Jersey	37	45	.451	17
New York	31	51	.378	23
Boston	29	53	.354	25

Central Division

* San Antonio	48	34	.585	—
* Houston	47	35	.573	1
* Atlanta	46	36	.561	2
Cleveland	30	52	.366	18
Detroit	30	52	.366	18
New Orleans	26	56	.317	22

WESTERN CONFERENCE

Midwest Division

* Kansas City	48	34	.585	—
* Denver	47	35	.573	1
Indiana	38	44	.463	10
Milwaukee	38	44	.463	10
Chicago	31	51	.378	17

Pacific Division

* Seattle	52	30	.634	—
* Phoenix	50	32	.610	2
* Los Angeles	47	35	.573	5
* Portland	45	37	.554	7
San Diego	43	39	.524	9
Golden State	38	44	.463	14

17

THE 1979 PLAYOFFS

THE BLAZERS were clear underdogs in their opening playoff best two of three battle against the Phoenix Suns. The Suns had strengthened an already strong squad with a midseason trade that brought rebounder and scorer Truck Robinson from the New Orleans Jazz. Joining Robinson on the front line were superlative center Alvin Adams and 1978 Rookie of the Year Walter Davis. In the backcourt, Paul Westphal was one of the premier scorers in the NBA, and his partner Don Buse was a player with unmatched defensive skills. The strong starting squad was backed up by a strong bench, and the Suns had compiled the third best record in the NBA.

Portland's primary advantage against the Suns was size on the front line. With a starting front court of Lucas, Owens, and Thompson, the Blazers figured to keep Phoenix from the offensive boards and contest enough rebounds on their own end to slow the Phoenix fast break. This board dominance was essential, for the Blazers' ability to stop Davis and Westphal, the Suns' two top guns, was very much in question. Since Bob Gross was out for the series, the Blazers had no top defensive small forward to check the lightning-quick Davis. With Hollins impaired by injury, the rookie Brewer would have to do his best against Westphal.

The opening game of the series, played at Phoenix on April 10, was a seesaw battle all the way. As expected, the Blazers dominated the boards, eventually outrebounding Phoenix 45–30. For the Suns, Davis and Westphal were magnificent. In the last quarter, the two Phoenix stars scored the last 17 points for their team. Although the Blazers only allowed Phoenix four offensive rebounds, one of them came with three seconds left and the Suns were up by two points. Adams slipped through the Portland players to grab a missed shot by Don Buse, then passed out to Walter Davis for a jumper that made the final score 107–103. For the Blazers, Ron Brewer had 26 points, two short of Westphal's 28, but Walter Davis had 25.

Game Two at Portland three nights later was another seesaw battle, but this time Portland emerged victorious. Again the Blazers led in rebounding, and again Walter Davis had a great game, scoring 31 points. But Ron Brewer tossed in 21 and held Westphal to 18. Cleamon Johnson, filling for foul-plagued Tom Owens, was a tower of strength defensively in the middle. The crucial 96–92 Portland triumph sent the series to the final game, to be played April 16 in Phoenix.

For three quarters of that last game the Blazers played magnificent basketball. With a 76–68 lead at the end of three quarters, an upset seemed imminent. But the Blazer lead obscured the crucial fact that for the first time the Suns' front line was outrebounding the Blazers. With the rebounding edge, it was only a matter of time before the Phoenix offense got untracked. At the start of the fourth quarter, Phoenix reeled off 14 straight points, outscored the Blazers 33–15 for the period, and won the game and

The Pride of Portland

the series 101–91. But the Portland team went home proud of its gutsy effort. Outgunned offensively, hampered by injuries to two remaining starters from the championship team, starting two rookies against a veteran team, the Blazers produced an impressive display of team basketball. Once again, in adversity, the team proved capable of embracing the tenets that brought them a championship just two years before. If they were no longer a championship team, they remained a championship franchise.

The prospects for the future looked bright. The 1979 college draft brought a talented, rugged big guard, Jim Paxson, from Dayton. Paxson's shooting ability is tailor-made for the new three-point rule in effect for the 1979–80 NBA season. Further quality ballplayers will come to Portland when Commissioner Larry O'Brian decides on the compensation from San Diego for the signing of Bill Walton. Scoring punch and depth added to the present talent means strong contending teams for years to come.

APPENDIX I

The Trail Blazers Year by Year

1970-71

*I*N 1970 the NBA expanded, adding the Buffalo Braves, the Cleveland Cavaliers, and the Portland Trail Blazers, and split into four divisions. The New York Knickerbockers, led by league MVP Willis Reed, were the defending NBA champions; Milwaukee, now with Oscar Robertson and Lew Alcindor, and the Los Angeles Lakers with all-time greats Jerry West, Elgin Baylor, and Wilt Chamberlain figured to be the best teams in the league. Heralded rookies entering the league included Pistol Pete Maravich from LSU, Bob Lanier from St. Bonaventure, and Dave Cowens from Florida State.

Portland joined the Pacific Division, which included Los Angeles, Seattle, the then San Francisco Warriors, and the San Diego Rockets. One of the biggest early season NBA rumors was that the enigmatic Howard Hughes wanted to buy the Boston Celtics and move them to Las Vegas, Nevada. There were no rumors around the league that any of the three expansion teams would be in any way, shape, or form dangerous—or even competitive.

Phil Elderkin, writing in *The Sporting News* basketball preview issue, flatly declared that "the only trail the Trail Blazers will blaze this year is one of frustration. It's going to be a long season." Coach Rolland Todd (called Mod Todd for his propensity to wear "flamboyant" bell-bottom pants—compared to Jack Ramsay's current dress Todd looked like a Wall Street banker) assembled a team that had veteran Leroy Ellis (from the Baltimore Bullets) at center, a weak collection of forwards including Ed Manning, Dorie Murray, Dale Schleuter, Jerry Chambers, and Gary Gregor among others, and a respectable guard crew of Jim Barnett (who had averaged 14.9 points per game for San Diego), Rick Adelman, Stan McKenzie, and top rookie Geoff Petrie from Princeton. (Jack Ramsay, with more hair, was coach of the 76ers led by top scorer and rebounder Billy Cunningham).

In their first game ever Portland defeated a hapless Cleveland team 115–112, Petrie, Barnett, and McKenzie combining for 71 points. For the Cavaliers it was the start of a 15-game losing streak which tied the previous league worst set by the old 1949–50 Denver Nuggets. Cleveland coach Bill Fitch in early December said, "I was 37 when the season started and I don't think I'm more than five or six years older now." With the Blazers off to a 5–7 start coach Todd said, "I'm tickled to death with the way we've played. We can't play any better."

But despite the long jump shots of Geoff Petrie, who averaged 24.8 points per game and became only the seventh rookie in league history to score 2,000 points and was later named Co-Rookie of the Year (with Dave Cowens), the Blazers ended up dead last in the Pacific Division with a 29–53 record, 19 games behind the division-winning L.A.

The Pride of Portland

Lakers. Only high scorer Petrie, McKenzie, and Ellis, who led the team in assists and rebounding respectively, plus Barnett, played NBA-caliber basketball. Gary Gregor showed promise. Most of the others did not. Of some solace was the fact that Portland had a significantly better record than its two expansion team brethren—Buffalo and Cleveland, who wound up 22–60 and 15–67 respectively. Fitch spoke for all the expansion clubs when he stated at season's end: "I feel so low I could hang myself on a curbstone."

Cleveland had only one reason for elation the entire season: a coin toss victory over Portland for the right to choose first in the NBA college draft. They promptly failed to capitalize on the advantage by bypassing Sidney Wicks to take high-scoring Notre Dame guard Austin Carr, who still has yet to make his mark in the NBA. Portland was "surprised and delighted" to find Wicks available, quickly choosing and signing the quick UCLA forward. Curtis Rowe, Darnell Hillman, Fred Brown, and Jim Cleamons were some of the other names available in this lackluster draft year.

Another reason for cautious optimism for Portland fans was the team's offense, a division-leading 115.1 points per game. Unfortunately the defense was the worst in the division, allowing an astounding 120 points per game.

At season's end as the Bucks rolled over the Bullets in four straight to the championship of the NBA, Blazer Pres-

1970–71 FINAL STANDINGS

PACIFIC DIVISION

Los Angeles	48	34	.585	—
San Francisco	41	41	.500	7
San Diego	40	42	.488	8
Seattle	38	44	.463	10
PORTLAND	29	53	.354	19

ident Herman Sarkowsky said: "We're here to stay." Another place the Blazers were destined to stay was last place.

1971-72

The Blazers' second season began poorly, and continued that way for the entire season. Leroy Ellis and Jim Barnett had been traded for draft picks to Los Angeles and San Francisco respectively, leaving the team weak at guard and center, and Geoff Petrie hurt his knee, requiring surgery and virtually ensuring a bad start for the team.

Billy Smith, a big center from Syracuse, won the starting nod over Dale Schleuter, Wicks and Gary Gregor were the starting forwards, and Rick Adelman, Stan McKenzie, and a rookie from Fordham, Charley Yelverton, shared guard duties. It was a team that would get off to a 1-5 start and by November 27, at 2-11 (.154), would already find itself ten full games behind the L.A. Lakers, who despite the retirement of the great Elgin Baylor were in the process of putting together one of the longest win streaks in professional sports history—finally winding up with 28 in a row.

Sidney Wicks continued to play well, but as Abdul-Jabbar said at the time, "he can't do it all by himself." Petrie returned in the first week of December, even scored 35 points in his second game, but the Blazers were a hapless team even with his scoring. By December 18 the record was 4-21, the worst in the NBA, and they were 18½ games behind the Lakers! Meanwhile the Milwaukee Bucks and the Lakers at the same time stood 23-4 and 23-3 respectively. To make matters worse, Bill Smith, who had shown real pro potential, injured his knee the night Petrie returned; he never played a regular season game again.

The 1971-72 NBA season became a war between two great superpowers: the Bucks led by Jabbar, Robertson,

John McGlothen, and Bob Dandridge and the Lakers led by Chamberlain, West, Gail Goodrich, and Happy Hairston. Leroy Ellis played very well for the Lakers and coach Bill Sharman commented: "We owe a debt of gratitude to Portland for practically giving us Leroy Ellis." The only bright spot for the Blazers was the play of young Sid Wicks, who led the team in scoring and rebounding— winding up the season with 24.5 points per game 11.5 rebounds per game.

Wicks was selected an all-star and praise around the league was lavish for the promising youngster. Coach Earl Lloyd of the Detroit Pistons said: "If I asked God to send me down a forward, he would send me Sidney Wicks." Bill Bridges, the veteran forward of the 76ers, said: "Nothing he does surprises me. He's just a great athlete, with fantastic skills." Wicks finished the season in the league's top twenty in scoring and rebounding—only two forwards, John Havlicek and Bill Cunningham, had better statistical seasons as NBA forwards. Still criticism was common; criticism which Wicks felt bitterly about. "I can't turn any team around," he said at one point. "I don't know what people expect of me. Basketball is a five-man game."

In February with the team clearly playing the worst basketball in the league, and its two stars Petrie and Wicks reportedly feuding, management decided to fire Rolland Todd. Stu Inman took over for the rest of the season. Rookie Larry Steele, under Inman, saw much more playing time and showed promise for the future with his accurate shooting and ball hawking defense. Final standings found Portland with a 18–64 record (.220), 51 games behind the Lakers, who finished 69–13 (The Bucks finished 65–19.) The team was the worst in basketball, and finished last in the division in both offense and defense, 106.8 and 116.5 points per game respectively.

Portland chose first in the 1972 NBA college draft and

picked LaRue Martin of Chicago Loyola. The team had wanted Bob McAdoo of North Carolina but was scared away by reports that he had already signed with the ABA. With the two picks they received in compensation for Jim Barnett the Blazers struck gold, choosing Dave Twardzik and Lloyd Neal. The Leroy Ellis deal resulted in the Blazers picking Ollie Johnson.

Despite the horrible season record the Blazer attendance jumped to an average of 6,988, nearly doubling from the previous year and placing the franchise tenth overall in the NBA.

Other than Wicks and Petrie (the two together somewhat of a mixed blessing), and the fans' enthusiasm, there was precious little to cheer about during the long, dreadful season.

1971-72 FINAL STANDINGS

PACIFIC DIVISION

Los Angeles	69	13	.841	—
Golden State	51	31	.622	18
Seattle	47	35	.573	22
Houston	34	48	.415	35
PORTLAND	18	64	.220	51

1972-73

Bob Wolf wrote in *Sporting News'* preview issue that "the only thing certain in the Pacific Division for the 1972-73 season are the Blazers—they'll finish last. The only consolation for Blazer fans is it can't be as bad as last year."

It wasn't; the Blazers won three more games than the previous year under new head coach Jack McCloskey. And the season started as badly as last year's, the Blazers crawling to a 1-10 record; by December 2 the team was 4-12 and already 10½ games behind the powerful Lakers. Only the 76ers—perhaps the worst team in basketball history—at 1-19 and the Buffalo Sabers at 3-15 had poorer records.

Rookie "sleeper" Lloyd Neal won the starting center job from first-pick LaRue Martin and performed excellently, despite at 6'7" giving up a great deal in height to the rest of the NBA centers. It didn't seem to affect Neal; in one early season game he burned Wilt Chamberlain for 25 points. Martin was a big disappointment. Though a decent shooter and ball handler, he proved too skinny and too timid to play evenly against most NBA centers. The other starters, Petrie, Wicks, Neal, and Ollie Johnson, formed a solid if unspectacular nucleus; the team needed a center.

At season's end Bob McAdoo, with his prolific scoring, was named Rookie of the Year; Lloyd Neal was second in the voting. Portland and Philadelphia, with the worst records in the Eastern and Western Divisions of the NBA, flipped for first pick in the draft and Philadelphia won. Said Wolf in *Sporting News:* "No team in the 27 year history of the NBA deserved it [the first pick] more." The 76ers ended the season with a 9-73 record; Portland and Cleveland tied at 21-61 and coexpansion club Buffalo wound up 32-50 (under Jack Ramsay). Petrie was seventh in the league in scoring (24.9) and Wicks was ninth (23.8); Neal led the team in rebounding with an 11.8 average. The team finished fourth in the division in offense (106.2) and fourth in defense (112.4).

Portland traded the right to pick second in the college draft to Cleveland, where Bill Fitch badly wanted Minnesota's Jim Brewer. In return the Blazers received John Johnson, Rick Roberson, and Cleveland's first-round pick with which they chose Virginia's star guard Barry Parkhill. Said Coach McCloskey: "Parkhill has unlimited potential in this league." He never scored a point for the Blazers.

In the NBA championships the Knicks shocked the L.A. Lakers to win the championship.

Blazer attendance was, improbably, up again. Phil Elderkin in *Sporting News* said, "Sidney Wicks is the chief reason Portland is still in the NBA."

1972–73 FINAL STANDINGS

PACIFIC DIVISION

Los Angeles	60	22	.732	—
Golden State	47	35	.573	13
Phoenix	38	44	.463	22
Seattle	26	56	.317	34
PORTLAND	21	61	.256	39

1973–74

For the first time the club opened the season with a set lineup of seasoned professionals: Rick Roberson at center, Sidney Wicks and John Johnson at forward, Petrie and Larry Steele at guard. Lloyd Neal to back up ably at either center or forward. The Blazers, again under Jack McCloskey, got off to a 3–0 start and in mid-November, with a record of 7–5, the team was heralded as the "most improved in the NBA."

The team gradually dropped below .500 but as late as January 26 with a record of 19–24 the Blazers were in third place, only 3½ games behind the league-leading Lakers. The season also saw the first Blazer victory—ever—over the Lakers, the last team in the NBA that the team had not beaten.

But January and February proved disastrous months, the team going 2–11 and 2–14, and any hope of real improvement ended. Coach McCloskey, showing the frustration, attempted to break up a fight between Chicago's Jerry Sloan and Wicks and wound up fighting Sloan at midcourt himself. Wicks did his part throughout the season, and at one point had a remarkable string of 30 consecutive games in which he scored 20 or more points. But the team de-

The Pride of Portland

fense was poor, the rebounding unsteady, the teamwork often nonexistent.

The Blazers wound up a season that started so well with the second worst record in the league again; only hapless Philadelphia was worse. The 27–55 record, though an improvement of six games, was still worse than both Cleveland (29–53) and Buffalo (42–40). The offense (106.8) was last in the Pacific Division, as was the defense (111.6).

Two new bright spots: John Johnson's scoring (16.4 points per game) and ball handling, plus the defense of Steele, who led the NBA in steals (2.68 a game)—the first league leadership in any statistical category for the Blazers.

At the end of the season the franchise's first big break occurred: in a coin flip for the rights to draft first and select, of course, Bill Walton, the Blazers lucked out. Walton was theirs. Already the only team in the division with two all-stars—Wicks and Petrie—Portland looked to a brand-new future.

1973–74 FINAL STANDINGS

PACIFIC DIVISION

Los Angeles	47	35	.573	—
Golden State	44	38	.537	3
Seattle	36	46	.437	11
Phoenix	30	52	.366	17
PORTLAND	27	55	.329	20

1974–75

The first Walton season. Sidney Wicks said: "We don't need Walton to score big. We have a lot of firepower on this club." New coach Lenny Wilkens, who decided to play for another season as well, had a strong nucleus of scorers (Wicks, Petrie, J. Johnson), rebounders (Walton, Neal, Wicks), and defenders (Walton, Steele, Neal), he could juggle. The Lakers lost Jerry West to retirement, and the Blazers lost a prime nemesis.

In the early season Walton led the league in rebounding and blocked shots (Jabbar had broken his hand in a temper tantrum by slamming it against a basket support), and was scoring in the mid-teens, bearing out Wicks's contention that the team could win (12–10 as of December 1) without big points from Walton.

But then Walton's injuries started and between a broken little finger and painful bone spurs (for which Walton will not take pain-killers), he missed almost two months. Portland went 3–9 without Walton in December.

In February, with Walton missing games, the team record was 4–10. Rumors abounded that Walton did not want to play basketball in Portland. Walton denied them all, saying the rumors were "a gross misunderstanding. I love Portland." The rookie showed flashes of brilliance but his sporadic play caused team morale problems and when the sky-high expectations for the season were not realized, both players and fans alike wondered what Walton was all about. In retrospect the problem seemed simple: injury. In his rookie year Bill Walton only played in 35 games; perhaps half of those at peak form. When he was healthy the team won.

At season's end, despite the clamor both pro and con, the Blazers had an almost respectable record of 38–44; for the first time the team did not finish in the Pacific Division cellar, finishing third instead. Wicks led the team in scoring with 21.7 points per game and in rebounding with 10.7 per game. He shot almot 50 percent from the floor and statistically had a fine all-around season. Still he and prolific scorer Geoff Petrie were not getting along and the Blazers were plainly a team riddled with dissension. But progress was made. Lloyd Neal played excellently. As a starter at center he averaged 21 points per game and 11 rebounds. The team finished first in the division in defense (103.3 points per game), a complete turnaround from the previous year, and second in offense (103.8). The Blazers led the entire NBA in field goal percentage (.480) and for the first time ever in final season statistics outscored, outshot, outrebounded, and outassisted its opponents. With a healthy Bill Walton, and despite personality conflicts, it was a team that could have been a contender for the NBA championship.

But Lenny Wilkens remained dissatisfied. "We simply did not play with intelligence or consistency and we can't go through another season like this. The players we have could complement one another, and if they can't realize this we'll have to make some changes."

1974–75 FINAL STANDINGS

PACIFIC DIVISION

Golden State	48	34	.585	—
Seattle	43	39	.524	5
PORTLAND	38	44	.463	10
Phoenix	32	50	.390	16
Los Angeles	30	52	.366	18

1975–76

Rookie Lionel Hollins joined the Blazers in 1975 and immediately proved himself an enormous asset; only an appendectomy operation kept him from starting the first game of the season. His fine defensive play at guard was desperately needed. Big Bill Walton arrived at training camp weighing 251 pounds, his most ever, but immediately ran into more injuries including bruised legs from an auto accident, a broken toe, and an eye injury.

Wilkens, who retired to end his illustrious playing career, started a club, or rather wanted to, when everyone was healthy, of Walton, Wicks, Neal, Hollins, and Petrie,

The Pride of Portland

with Steele and John Johnson as excellent reserves. But Johnson, who had started the entire previous year, strongly objected, and two games into the season demanded to be traded, finally getting his wish in a deal for Steve Hawes of Houston. His defection hurt the team's depth.

In the first game of the season Walton and John Hummer of Seattle exchanged blows and both were ejected. The next night an angry Walton scored his pro high of 33 points and grabbed 18 rebounds, though Portland lost to Phoenix anyway. The team lost its first four games, its worst start ever, and Wilkens said, "We really got down after those losses because we all felt we're a better club than that. The thing that hurts about the injuries is that we're still a young club and need the work together."

That consistent "work" was never realized. Walton suffered from bone spurs, a broken left wrist, and dislocated fingers. Steele also had bone spurs. The young team led the league in turnovers. Teamwork worsened as injuries and losses mounted. In December the team went 4–10, in February 6–8; then Walton's ankle was put in a cast, and though the team played .500 ball for the rest of the season without him, the year once again was frustratingly futile.

Away from home the Blazers were 11–30; at home 26–15. The 37–45 record represented a drop of one game from the previous year even though Walton played in 16 more games. The team resumed its accustomed spot at the bottom of the Pacific Division. Wicks led the team in scoring with 19.1 points per game and Petrie was second at 18.9. Walton led in rebounding average with 13.3. The Blazers were last in the division in offense (104.1) and third in defense (105.3). Hollins showed great promise, averaging 10.8 points per game, and Lloyd Neal had his finest season, averaging 15.5 points per game.

Attendance rose over 2,000 spectators per game for an average of 12,178; but for the first time the crowds were

The Pride of Portland

booing the Blazers. A season that began with much hope ended in dissension and disappointment. It was obvious that massive changes had to be made.

Those changes were made, and the next season began a period of success for franchise—and for fans—that had done little but suffer for six long years.

1975-76 FINAL STANDINGS

PACIFIC DIVISION

Golden State	59	23	.720	—
Seattle	43	39	.524	16
Phoenix	42	40	.512	17
Los Angeles	40	42	.488	19
PORTLAND	37	45	.451	22

APPENDIX II

Portland Trail Blazer Statistics

ALL-TIME RECORD

Season	Home	Road	Neutral	Total
1970–71	18-21	9-26	2-6	29-53
1971–72	14-26	4-35	0-3	18-64
1972–73	13-28	8-32	0-1	21-61
1973–74	22-19	5-34	0-2	27-55
1974–75	28-13	10-31	0-0	38-44
1975–76	26-15	11-30	0-0	37-45
1976–77	35-6	14-27	0-0	49-33
1977–78	36-5	22-19	0-0	58-24
1978–79	33-8	12-29	0-0	45-37

ALL-TIME OFFENSIVE RECORDS

Season	GP	FGM	FGA	PCT	FTM	FTA	PCT	REB	AST	PF	PTS	AVE
1970–71	82	3731	8562	.435	2025	2671	.758	4210	2227	2024	9467	115.5
1971–72	82	3462	7840	.442	1835	2494	.736	3996	2090	1873	8759	106.8
1972–73	82	3588	7842	.458	1531	2129	.719	3928	2109	1970	8707	106.2
1973–74	82	3585	7684	.467	1591	2112	.753	3852	2106	2050	8761	106.8
1974–75	82	3414	7113	.480	1680	2265	.742	3809	2209	2055	8508	103.8
1975–76	82	3417	7292	.469	1699	2350	.723	3959	2094	2091	8533	104.1
1976–77	82	3621	7537	.480	1917	2515	.762	3963	1990	2220	9163	111.7
1977–78	82	3556	7367	.483	1717	2259	.760	3873	2067	2068	8829	107.7
1978–79	82	3541	7338	.483	1806	2501	.765	3691	1946	2187	8888	108.4

ALL-TIME DEFENSE RECORDS

Season	GP	FGM	FGA	PCT	FTM	FTA	PCT	REB	AST	PF	PTS	AVE
1970–71	82	3900	8333	.468	2037	2758	.739	4885	2267	2065	9837	120.0
1971–72	82	3841	7906	.486	1875	2499	.750	4439	2312	1903	9557	116.5
1972–73	82	3709	7780	.477	1800	2327	.774	4236	2271	1885	9218	112.4
1973–74	82	3664	7571	.484	1825	2299	.794	3875	2308	1961	9153	111.6
1974–75	82	3379	7502	.450	1714	2178	.787	3778	2090	2085	8472	103.3
1975–76	82	3405	7531	.452	1825	2333	.782	3778	1920	2128	8635	105.3
1976–77	82	3408	7404	.460	1889	2514	.751	3707	1817	2242	8705	106.1
1977–78	82	3289	7318	.449	1747	2282	.766	3710	1818	2096	8325	101.5
1978–79	82	3448	7059	.488	1889	2501	.755	3430	1963	2206	8785	107.1

The Pride of Portland

ALL-TIME LEADERS

GAMES PLAYED		MINUTES PLAYED		POINTS		REBOUNDS	
Steele	594	Petrie	16,787	Petrie	9,732	Wicks	4,086
Petrie	446	Wicks	15,456	Wicks	8,882	Neal	3,370
Neal	435	Steele	14,331	Steele	4,853	Walton	2,822
Wicks	398	Neal	10,955	Neal	4,846	Lucas	2,236
Hollins	295	Hollins	8,823	Hollins	4,180	Steele	1,737
Gross	283	Lucas	7,444	Lucas	4,118	Schlueter	1,510
Martin	271	Gross	7,310	Walton	3,578	Gross	1,351
Adelman	237	Walton	7,033	Gross	2,878	Owens	1,281
Lucas	235	Adelman	6,570	J. Johnson	2,527	Petrie	1,271
Twardzik	213	Twardzik	5,327	Owens	2,352	Martin	1,256

FREE THROWS ATTEMPTED		FREE THROWS MADE		FIELD GOALS ATTEMPTED		FIELD GOALS MADE	
Wicks	2,634	Wicks	1,878	Petrie	8,719	Petrie	3,970
Petrie	2,225	Petrie	1,792	Wicks	7,605	Wicks	3,502
Neal	1,316	Steele	947	Neal	4,087	Neal	1,981
Steele	1,191	Neal	884	Steele	4,034	Steele	1,958
Hollins	1,055	Lucas	812	Hollins	3,872	Hollins	1,676
Lucas	1,053	Hollins	788	Lucas	3,556	Lucas	1,654
Walton	938	Twardzik	683	Walton	2,889	Walton	1,473
Twardzik	817	McKenzie	660	Gross	2,274	Gross	1,175
McKenzie	791	Walton	632	Adelman	2,173	J. Johnson	1,027
Owens	681	Gross	528	J. Johnson	2,160	Adelman	921

ASSISTS		PERSONAL FOULS	
Petrie	2,027	Steele	1,779
Steele	1,652	Neal	1,271
Wicks	1,647	Wicks	1,192
Hollins	1,324	Petrie	1,075
Adelman	1,087	Hollins	967
Walton	923	Gross	836
Gross	843	Lucas	772
Twardzik	667	Martin	617
Neal	632	Twardzik	599
Lucas	617	Owens	592

The Pride of Portland

ALL-TIME RECORDS—REGULAR SEASON

FULL GAME

Most Points	Geoff Petrie	Portland at Houston	1-20-73	51
	Geoff Petrie	Houston at Portland	3-16-73	51
Most FGA	Geoff Petrie	Portland at Golden State	2- 8-73	37
Most FGM	Geoff Petrie	Portland at Golden State	2- 8-73	20
	Geoff Petrie	Portland at Philadelphia	3-20-74	20
	Lionel Hollins	Boston at Portland	2-22-77	20
Most FTA	Geoff Petrie	Seattle at Portland	3-19-71	21
Most FTM	Geoff Petrie	Seattle at Portland	3-19-71	18
Most Rebounds	Sidney Wicks	Portland at Los Angeles	2-26-75	27
Most Assists	Rick Adelman	Cleveland at Portland	11-19-71	17
Most Steals	Larry Steele	Los Angeles at Portland	11-16-74	10
Most BS	Bill Walton	Portland at Golden State	10-22-74	9

ONE HALF

Most Points	Geoff Petrie	Portland at Philadelphia	3-20-74	30
Most FGA	LeRoy Ellis	Detroit at Portland	3-12-71	20
	Geoff Petrie	Portland at Golden State	2- 8-73	20
	Geoff Petrie	Portland at Philadelphia	3-20-74	20
Most FGM	Geoff Petrie	Portland at Philadelphia	3-20-74	14
Most FTA	Sidney Wicks	Atlanta at Portland	10-24-72	15
Most FTM	Sidney Wicks	Atlanta at Portland	10-24-72	12
Most Rebounds	LeRoy Ellis	Philadelphia at Portland	2-20-71	16
	Bill Walton	Portland at Golden State	1-24-76	16
Most Assists	Rick Adelman	Cleveland at Portland	2-20-71	9
	Sidney Wicks	Phoenix at Portland	2- 5-71	9
Most Personals	Bill Smith	Milwaukee at Portland	11-16-71	6
	Darrall Imhoff	Portland at Houston	1-25-72	6
Most Steals	Larry Steele	Los Angeles at Portland	11-16-74	7
Most BS	Bill Walton	Portland at Denver	1-26-77	8

ONE QUARTER

Most Points	Geoff Petrie	Golden State at Portland	3-17-72	22
Most FGA	Geoff Petrie	Cleveland at Portland	2-21-71	12
	Sidney Wicks	Cincinnati at Portland	10-23-71	12
	Sidney Wicks	Golden State at Portland	3-17-72	12
Most FGM	Geoff Petrie	Cleveland at Portland	2-21-71	9
Most FTA	Sidney Wicks	Atlanta at Portland	10-24-72	10
Most FTM	Sidney Wicks	Atlanta at Portland	10-24-72	9
Most Rebounds	LeRoy Ellis	Portland at New York	12- 8-71	12
	LeRoy Ellis	Philadelphia at Portland	2-20-71	12
Most Assists	Rick Adelman	Portland at Chicago	12-30-71	7

The Pride of Portland

ALL-TIME TEAM RECORDS

FULL GAME

Most Points	San Antonio at Portland	1- 9-77	150
Most FGA	Three Games		125
Most FGM	Three Games		59
Most FTA	Two Games		60
Most FTM	Seattle at Portland	3- 5-77	46
Most Rebounds	Atlanta at Portland	11-18-70	78
Most Personals	Two Games		42
Most Assists	Atlanta at Portland	11-18-70	44
	Golden State at Portland	3-27-74	44
Most Steals	NY Knicks at Portland	11- 7-76	23
Most BS	Kansas City at Portland	2- 8-74	20

ONE HALF

Most Points	Atlanta at Portland	11-18-70	82
Most FGA	Atlanta at Portland	11-18-70	67
Most FGM	Two Games		32
Most FTA	Seattle at Portland	3- 5-77	41
Most FTM	Seattle at Portland	3- 5-77	31
Most Rebounds	New York at Portland	1- 9-71	43
Most Assists	Golden State at Portland	3-27-74	27
Most Personals	Portland at Atlanta	1-16-77	27
Most Steals	NY Knicks at Portland	11- 7-76	12

ONE QUARTER

Most Points	Boston at Portland	1- 3-76	49
Most FGA	Portland at Los Angeles	12- 6-70	41
Most FGM	Cleveland at Portland	2-21-71	20
Most FTA	Seattle at Portland	3- 5-77	27
Most FTM	Seattle at Portland	3- 5-77	21
Most Rebounds	Baltimore at Portland	3-11-71	27
Most Assists	Golden State at Portland	3-27-74	15
Most Personals	Portland at Atlanta	1-16-77	19
Most Steals	NY Knicks at Portland	11- 7-76	8

The Pride of Portland

ALL-TIME TOP TEN TRAIL BLAZERS' PERFORMANCE

POINTS

Geoff Petrie	Portland at Houston	1-20-73	51
Geoff Petrie	Houston at Portland	3-16-73	51
Geoff Petrie	Seattle at Portland	3-19-71	46
Maurice Lucas	Portland at Boston	1-12-79	46
Lionel Hollins	Boston at Portland	2-22-77	43
Geoff Petrie	Seattle at Portland	2-12-71	43
Geoff Petrie	Portland at Philadelphia	2-23-71	43
Geoff Petrie	Portland at Seattle	11-22-73	43
Geoff Petrie	Portland at Philadelphia	3-20-74	43
Geoff Petrie	Portland at Golden State	2- 8-73	42
Geoff Petrie	Portland at Detroit	3- 2-71	41
Geoff Petrie	Portland at Seattle	3-24-73	41
Maurice Lucas	Atlanta at Portland	2-11-77	41

REBOUNDS

Sidney Wicks	Portland at Los Angeles	2-26-75	27
Bill Walton	Portland at Golden State	12-30-77	26
Bill Walton	Los Angeles at Portland	12-18-76	26
Bill Walton	Portland at Golden State	1-24-76	26
LeRoy Ellis	Buffalo at Portland	10-27-70	26
Sidney Wicks	Golden State at Portland	1-28-72	25
LeRoy Ellis	Golden State at Portland	11-29-70	25
Bill Walton	Golden State at Portland	10-25-74	25
Bill Walton	Cleveland at Portland	10-18-74	24
Sidney Wicks	Golden State at Portland	3-17-72	23
Lloyd Neal	Portland at Los Angeles	10-28-73	23

The Pride of Portland

ALL-TIME TOP TEN TRAIL BLAZERS' PERFORMANCE

ASSISTS

Rick Adelman	Cleveland at Portland	11-19-71	17
Sidney Wicks	Buffalo at Portland	1- 1-74	14
Bill Walton	Seattle at Portland	2- 1-75	14
Geoff Petrie	Buffalo at Portland	3-16-75	14
Geoff Petrie	Golden State at Portland	3- 2-75	13
Rick Adelman	Atlanta at Portland	2- 4-71	13
Larry Steele	Chicago at Portland	11-14-75	13
Rick Adelman	Detroit at Portland	10-19-71	12
Jim Barnett	San Diego at Portland	12- 1-70	12
Sidney Wicks	Golden State at Portland	10-21-72	12
Rick Adelman	Atlanta at Portland	12 2-72	12
Sidney Wicks	Buffalo at Portland	11- 9-73	12
Sidney Wicks	Portland at Detroit	11 14-73	12
Geoff Petrie	KC-Omaha at Portland	1- 8-74	12
Geoff Petrie	Golden State at Portland	1-26-75	12
Lionel Hollins	Philadelphia at Portland	1-28-79	12

The Pride of Portland

JACK RAMSAY'S COACHING RECORD

ST. JOSEPH'S

Season	Won	Lost	Pct
1955–56	23	6	.793
1956–57	17	7	.708
1957–58	18	9	.667
1958–59	22	5	.815
1959–60	20	7	.714
1960–61	25	5	.833
1961–62	18	10	.643
1962–63	23	5	.821
1963–64	18	10	.643
1964–65	26	3	.897
1965–66	24	5	.828

PHILADELPHIA (NBA)

Season	Won	Lost	Pct
1968–69	55	27	.671
1969–70	42	40	.512
1970–71	47	35	.573
1971–72	30	52	.366

BUFFALO (NBA)

Season	Won	Lost	Pct
1972–73	21	61	.256
1973–74	42	40	.512
1974–75	49	33	.598
1975–76	46	36	.561

PORTLAND (NBA)

Season	Won	Lost	Pct
1976–77	49	33	.598
1977–78	58	24	.707
1978–79	45	37	.549

PLAYOFF SCORING—1977

	G	MIN	FGM	FGA	PCT	FTM	FTA	PCT	OFF	DEF	REB	AST	PF	ST	BS	PTS	AVE	Hi
Lucas	19	731	164	316	.519	75	101	.743	43	145	188	79	79	28	23	403	21.2	29
Walton	19	755	153	302	.507	39	57	.684	56	232	288	104	80	20	64	345	18.2	28
Hollins	19	682	134	321	.417	60	88	.682	13	39	52	85	74	47	5	328	17.3	31
Gross	19	583	110	186	.591	48	54	.889	49	63	112	80	84	32	15	268	14.1	26
Twardzik	14	354	55	93	.591	43	59	.729	4	20	24	39	47	16	2	153	10.9	19
Davis	16	436	65	133	.489	38	53	.717	10	23	33	52	32	28	3	168	10.5	25
Gilliam	18	295	53	123	.431	9	12	.750	7	13	20	32	29	13	1	115	6.4	24
Walker	10	83	20	36	.556	3	7	.429	2	5	7	8	20	3	0	43	4.3	10
Steele	18	261	26	70	.371	24	32	.750	12	15	27	18	30	9	0	76	4.2	14
Neal	19	206	30	63	.476	17	26	.654	21	49	70	17	34	2	3	77	4.1	13
Calhoun	12	94	13	25	.520	2	3	.667	6	8	14	4	16	4	2	28	2.3	6
Jones	19	105	15	32	.469	6	9	.667	8	15	23	9	24	4	4	36	1.9	9

PLAYOFF RECORD GAME BY GAME—1977

Game	Date	Where	Opp.	First	Second	Third	Fourth	OT	W-L	Score
1	4-12	Home	Chic	29-19	23-23	21-26	23-15	—	1-0	96- 83
2	4-15	Road	Chic	24-24	22-26	31-29	27-28	—	1-1	104-107
3	4-17	Home	Chic	27-21	30-25	23-29	26-23	—	2-1	106- 98
	Totals			80-64	75-74	75-84	76-66			306-288
					(PORTLAND WINS 2-1)					
4	4-20	Road	Den	23-25	27-20	27-26	24-29	—	3-1	101-100
5	4-22	Road	Den	30-24	21-28	30-33	29-36	—	3-2	110-121
6	4-24	Home	Den	28-25	26-23	27-32	29-26	—	4-2	110-106
7	4-26	Home	Den	32-24	22-22	24-30	27-20	—	5-2	105- 96
8	5- 1	Road	Den	20-27	28-27	29-29	24-18	4-13	5-3	105-114
9	5- 2	Home	Den	33-16	29-29	26-19	20-28	—	6-3	108- 92
	Totals			166-141	153-149	163-169	153-157	4-13		639-629
					(PORTLAND WINS 4-2)					
10	5- 6	Road	LA	33-22	28-21	27-31	33-35	—	7-3	121-109
11	5- 8	Road	LA	26-25	28-26	16-26	29-20	—	8-3	99- 97
12	5-10	Home	LA	36-29	18-24	19-22	29-22	—	9-3	102- 97
13	5-13	Home	LA	31-25	18-19	30-29	26-28	—	10-3	105-101
	Totals			126-101	92-90	92-108	117-105			427-404
					(PORTLAND WINS 4-0)					
14	5-22	Road	Phil	25-27	28-28	25-31	23-21	—	10-4	101-107
15	5-26	Road	Phil	26-31	17-30	21-20	25-26	—	10-5	89-107
16	5-29	Home	Phil	34-21	26-32	27-29	42-25	—	11-5	129-107
17	5-31	Home	Phil	29-16	28-30	41-21	32-31	—	12-5	130- 98
18	6- 3	Road	Phil	22-15	23-26	40-25	25-38	—	13-5	110-104
19	6- 5	Home	Phil	27-27	40-28	24-27	18-25	—	14-5	109-107
	Totals			163-137	162-174	178-153	165-166			688-630
					(PORTLAND WINS 4-2)					

Portland at home won 10 and lost 0.

PLAYOFF RESULTS—1978

Game	Date	Where	Opp.	1st	2nd	3rd	4th	OT	W-L	Score
1	4-18	Home	Seattle	34-23	19-23	22-33	22-25	—	0-1	95-104
2	4-21	Home	Seattle	20-30	20-19	30-32	26-22	—	1-1	96-93
3	4-23	Road	Seattle	25-20	18-24	19-27	22-28	—	1-2	84-99
4	4-26	Road	Seattle	28-28	29-17	24-28	17-27	—	1-3	98-100
5	4-30	Home	Seattle	25-13	27-21	27-23	34-32	—	2-3	113-89
6	5-1	Road	Seattle	22-26	27-29	20-20	25-30	—	2-4	94-105

PLAYOFF SCORING—1978

	GP	MIN	FGM	FGA	PCT	FTM	FTA	PCT	OFF REB	DEF REB	TOT REB	AST	PF	STL	TO	BS	PTS	AVE	Hi
Lucas	6	233	46	108	.426	11	19	.579	19	56	75	15	28	4	19	1	103	17.2	24
Hollins	6	223	40	89	.449	20	29	.690	5	24	29	33	21	7	19	0	100	16.7	35
Owens	6	200	38	69	.551	15	21	.714	13	26	39	26	30	5	7	7	91	15.2	31
Davis	6	201	35	76	.461	16	23	.696	6	7	10	13	15	1	11	3	86	14.3	23
Walton	2	49	11	18	.611	5	7	.714	5	17	22	4	1	3	6	3	27	13.5	17
Steele	6	191	25	60	.417	19	21	.905	8	18	26	14	22	7	12	2	69	11.5	17
Twardzik	6	108	11	23	.478	14	14	1.000	1	3	4	11	16	7	10	0	36	6.0	10
Calhoun	6	109	15	29	.517	4	7	.571	6	8	14	3	6	2	3	1	34	5.7	16
Neal	3	47	7	21	.333	1	1	1.000	2	9	11	2	5	0	6	4	15	5.0	9
Norwood	3	44	7	12	.583	1	1	1.000	1	3	4	4	11	0	2	1	15	5.0	13
Dunn	4	35	2	4	.500	0	0	.000	1	4	5	3	3	1	1	0	4	1.0	4

PLAYOFF RESULTS—1979

Game	Date	Where	Opp.	1st	2nd	3rd	4th	W-L	Score
1	4-10	Away	Phoenix	20-33	26-25	27-31	30-28	0-1	95-104
2	4-13	Home	Phoenix	25-24	27-26	21-26	23-16	1-1	96- 93
3	4-16	Away	Phoenix	22-24	28-23	26-21	15-33	1-2	91-101

PLAYOFF SCORING—1979

	G	MIN	FGM	FGA	PCT	FTM	FTA	PCT	OFF REB	DEF REB	TOT REB	AST	PF	DQ	ST	TO	BS	PTS	AVE	Hi
Thompson	3	121	27	54	.500	5	10	.500	9	22	31	6	11	0	2	5	5	59	19.7	23
Brewer	3	94	22	39	.564	9	13	.692	4	7	11	8	7	0	1	5	9	53	17.7	26
Steele	3	73	16	28	.571	8	9	.889	6	5	11	7	8	0	10	3	0	40	13.3	16
Owens	3	80	15	31	.484	5	8	.625	9	10	19	5	16	1	4	7	1	35	11.7	14
Lucas	3	104	14	41	.341	5	7	.714	2	30	32	18	12	0	3	11	1	33	11.0	16
Twardzik	3	77	7	14	.500	11	12	.917	4	3	7	10	14	0	5	9	0	25	8.3	11
Hollins	3	66	8	26	.308	5	7	.714	1	2	3	5	8	0	3	7	0	21	7.0	8
Johnson	3	47	4	11	.364	6	11	.545	5	12	17	2	5	0	2	7	4	14	4.7	8
Dunn	3	52	5	11	.455	0	0	—	2	4	6	4	7	0	5	1	0	10	3.3	4
Terrell	1	6	0	4	.000	0	0	—	0	2	2	0	0	0	0	0	0	0	0.0	0

The Pride of Portland

SEASON LEADERS

MINUTES PLAYED

		GP	MIN	AVE
1970–71	Petrie	82	3032	37.0
1971–72	Wicks	82	3245	39.6
1972–73	Wicks	80	3115	39.4
1973–74	Wicks	75	2853	38.0
1974–75	Wicks	82	3162	38.6
1975–76	Wicks	79	3034	38.4
1976–77	Lucas	79	2863	36.2
1977–78	Hollins	81	2741	33.8
1978–79	Owens	82	2791	34.0

FOUL SHOOTING

		FTM	FTA	PCT
1970–71	McKenzie	331	396	.836
1971–72	McKenzie	315	379	.831
1972–73	C. Davis	126	161	.783
1973–74	Petrie	291	341	.857
1974–75	Petrie	261	311	.839
1975–76	Petrie	277	334	.829
1976–77	Gross	183	215	.851
1977–78	Davis	188	227	.828
1978–79	Twardzik	261	299	.873

SHOOTING

		FGM	FGA	PCT
1970–71	Petrie	784	1770	.443
1970–71	Ellis	485	1095	.443
1971–72	McKenzie	410	834	.492
1972–73	O. Johnson	308	620	.497
1973–74	Petrie	740	1537	.481
1974–75	Wicks	692	1391	.497
1975–76	Steele	322	651	.495
1976–77	Gross	376	711	.529
1977–78	Gross	381	720	.529
1978–79	Owens	600	1095	.548

REBOUNDS

		GP	REB	AVE
1970–71	Ellis	74	907	12.3
1971–72	Wicks	82	943	11.5
1972–73	Neal	82	967	11.8
1973–74	Roberson	69	701	10.2
1974–75	Wicks	82	877	10.7
1975–76	Wicks	79	712	9.0
1976–77	Walton	65	934	14.4
1977–78	Walton	58	766	13.2
1978–79	Owens	82	740	9.0

ASSISTS

		GP	AST	AVE
1970–71	Petrie	82	390	4.8
1971–72	Adelman	80	413	5.2
1972–73	Wicks	80	440	5.5
1973–74	Wicks	75	326	4.3
1974–75	Petrie	80	424	5.3
1975–76	Petrie	72	330	4.6
1976–77	Hollins	76	313	4.1
1977–78	Hollins	81	380	4.7
1978–79	Hollins	64	325	5.1

SCORING

		GP	PTS	AVE
1970–71	Petrie	82	2031	24.8
1971–72	Wicks	82	2009	24.5
1972–73	Petrie	79	1970	24.9
1973–74	Petrie	73	1771	24.3
1974–75	Wicks	82	1778	21.9
1975–76	Wicks	79	1505	19.1
1976–77	Lucas	79	1599	20.2
1977–78	Hollins	81	1285	15.9
1978–79	Lucas	69	1406	20.4

PORTLAND RECORDS OF ALL TRAIL BLAZERS

	GP	MIN	FGM	FGA	PCT	FTM	FTA	PCT	REB	AST	PF	PTS	AVE
RICK ADELMAN—LOYOLA (L.A.)													
1970–71	81	2303	378	895	.422	267	369	.724	282	380	214	1023	12.6
1971–72	80	2445	329	753	.437	151	201	.751	229	413	209	809	10.1
1972–73	76	1822	214	525	.408	73	102	.716	157	294	155	501	6.6
DANNY ANDERSON—USC													
1974–75	43	453	47	105	.448	26	30	.867	29	81	44	120	2.8
1975–76	52	614	88	181	.486	51	61	.836	62	85	58	227	4.4
KIM ANDERSON—MISSOURI													
1978–79	21	224	24	77	.312	15	28	.536	45	15	42	63	3.0
JIM BARNETT—OREGON													
1970–71	78	2371	559	1283	.436	326	402	.811	376	323	189	1444	18.5
RON BREWER—ARKANSAS													
1978–79	81	2454	434	878	.494	210	256	.820	229	165	181	1078	13.3
CORKY CALHOUN—PENNSYLVANIA													
1976–77	70	743	85	183	.464	66	85	.776	144	35	123	236	3.4
1977–78	79	1370	175	365	.479	66	76	.868	215	87	141	416	5.3
BARRY CLEMENS—OHIO WESLEYAN													
1974–75	77	952	108	355	.473	45	60	.750	161	76	139	381	4.9
1975–76	49	443	70	143	.490	21	25	.886	70	23	57	171	3.5

BOB DAVIS—WEBER STATE

Year	G	Min	FGM	FGA	FG%	FTM	FTA	FT%	Reb	Ast	PF	Pts	Avg
1972-73	9	41	6	28	.214	4	6	.667	5	2	5	16	1.8

CHARLIE DAVIS—WAKE FOREST

Year	G	Min	FGM	FGA	FG%	FTM	FTA	FT%	Reb	Ast	PF	Pts	Avg
1972-73	69	1333	243	590	.412	126	161	.783	111	175	174	612	8.9
1973-74	8	90	14	40	.350	3	4	.750	11	11	7	31	3.9

JOHNNY DAVIS—DAYTON

Year	G	Min	FGM	FGA	FG%	FTM	FTA	FT%	Reb	Ast	PF	Pts	Avg
1976-77	79	1451	234	531	.441	166	209	.794	126	148	128	634	8.0
1977-78	82	2188	343	756	.454	188	227	.828	173	217	173	874	10.7

TERRY DISCHINGER—PURDUE

Year	G	Min	FGM	FGA	FG%	FTM	FTA	FT%	Reb	Ast	PF	Pts	Avg
1972-73	63	970	161	338	.476	64	96	.667	190	103	125	386	6.1

JACKEY DORSEY—GEORGIA

Year	G	Min	FGM	FGA	FG%	FTM	FTA	FT%	Reb	Ast	PF	Pts	Avg
1977-78	4	51	9	19	.474	7	11	.636	10	3	8	25	6.3

T. R. DUNN—ALABAMA

Year	G	Min	FGM	FGA	FG%	FTM	FTA	FT%	Reb	Ast	PF	Pts	Avg
1977-78	63	768	100	240	.417	37	56	.661	147	45	74	237	3.8
1978-79	80	1828	246	381	.418	122	158	.772	344	103	166	614	7.7

LEROY ELLIS—ST. JOHN'S

Year	G	Min	FGM	FGA	FG%	FTM	FTA	FT%	Reb	Ast	PF	Pts	Avg
1970-71	74	2581	485	1095	.443	209	261	.801	907	235	258	1179	15.9

CLAUDE ENGLISH—RHODE ISLAND

Year	G	Min	FGM	FGA	FG%	FTM	FTA	FT%	Reb	Ast	PF	Pts	Avg
1970-71	18	70	11	42	.262	5	7	.714	20	6	15	27	1.5

BERNIE FRYER—BRIGHAM YOUNG

1973-74	80	1674	226	491	.460	107	135	.793	159	279	187	559	7.0

HERMAN GILLIAM—PURDUE

| 1976-77 | 80 | 1665 | 326 | 744 | .438 | 92 | 120 | .767 | 201 | 170 | 168 | 744 | 9.3 |

WALT GILMORE—FORT VALLEY STATE

| 1970-71 | 27 | 261 | 23 | 54 | .426 | 12 | 26 | .462 | 73 | 12 | 49 | 58 | 2.1 |

GARY GREGOR—SOUTH CAROLINA

| 1970-71 | 44 | 1153 | 181 | 421 | .430 | 59 | 89 | .663 | 334 | 81 | 120 | 421 | 9.6 |
| 1971-72 | 82 | 2371 | 399 | 884 | .451 | 114 | 151 | .755 | 591 | 187 | 201 | 912 | 11.1 |

BOB GROSS—LONG BEACH STATE

1975-76	76	1474	209	400	.523	97	142	.683	307	163	186	515	6.8
1976-77	82	2232	376	711	.529	183	215	.851	394	242	255	935	11.4
1977-78	72	2163	381	720	.529	152	190	.800	400	254	234	914	12.7
1978-79	53	1441	209	443	.472	96	119	.807	250	184	161	514	9.7

SHALER HALIMON—UTAH STATE

| 1970-71 | 79 | 1629 | 300 | 775 | .87 | 107 | 161 | .665 | 415 | 211 | 178 | 707 | 8.9 |

STEVE HAWES—WASHINGTON

| 1975-76 | 72 | 1411 | 199 | 403 | .494 | 87 | 120 | .725 | 497 | 115 | 169 | 485 | 6.7 |

LIONEL HOLLINS—ARIZONA STATE									
1975-76	74	1891	311	738	.421	178	.721	175	306	253	800	10.8
1976-77	76	2224	452	1046	.432	215	.749	210	313	265	1119	14.7
1977-78	81	2741	531	1202	.442	223	.743	277	380	268	1285	15.9
1978-79	64	1967	402	886	.454	172	.778	149	325	199	976	15.3
DARRALL IMHOFF—CALIFORNIA									
1971-72	40	404	42	103	.408	21	.600	107	50	76	105	2.6
CLEAMON JOHNSON—FLORIDA A&M									
1978-79	74	794	102	217	.470	36	.486	226	78	121	240	3.2
JOHN JOHNSON—IOWA									
1973-74	69	2287	459	990	.464	212	.812	515	284	221	1130	16.4
1974-75	80	2540	527	1082	.487	236	.784	501	240	249	1290	16.1
1975-76	9	212	41	88	.466	23	.852	40	20	31	107	11.7
OLLIE JOHNSON—TEMPLE									
1972-73	78	2138	308	620	.497	156	.757	206	417	200	166	772	9.9
1973-74	79	1718	209	434	.482	77	.819	94	324	167	179	495	6.3
ROBIN JONES—ST. LOUIS									
1976-77	63	1065	139	299	.465	66	.606	109	296	80	124	344	5.5
STEVE JONES—OREGON									
1975-76	64	819	168	380	.442	78	.830	94	75	63	96	414	6.5

RON KNIGHT—LOS ANGELES STATE

1970–71	52	662	99	230	.430	19	38	.500	167	50	99	217	4.2
1971–72	49	483	112	257	.436	31	62	.500	116	33	52	255	5.2

DENNIS LAYTON—USC

1973–74	22	327	55	112	.491	14	26	.538	33	51	45	124	5.6

GREG LEE—UCLA

1975–76	5	35	2	4	.500	2	2	1.000	2	11	6	6	1.2

MAURICE LUCAS—MARQUETTE

1976–77	79	2863	632	1359	.465	335	438	.765	899	229	294	1599	20.2
1977–78	68	2119	453	989	.458	207	270	.767	621	173	221	1113	16.4
1978–79	69	2462	568	1208	.471	270	345	.783	716	215	254	1406	20.4

PHIL LUMPKIN—MIAMI (OHIO)

1974–75	48	792	86	190	.453	30	39	.769	59	177	80	202	4.2

ED MANNING—JACKSON STATE

1970–71	79	1558	243	559	.435	75	93	.806	411	111	198	561	7.1

JIM MARSH—USC

1971–72	39	375	39	117	.333	41	59	.695	84	30	50	119	3.1

LARUE MARTIN—LOYOLA (CHICAGO)

1972–73	77	996	145	366	.396	50	77	.649	358	42	162	340	4.4
1973–74	50	538	101	232	.435	42	66	.636	181	20	90	244	4.9
1974–75	81	1372	236	522	.452	99	142	.697	408	69	239	571	7.0
1975–76	63	889	109	302	.361	57	77	.740	311	72	126	275	4.4

CLYDE MAYES—FURMAN

Year											
1976-77	5	24	2	9	.222	0	0	.000	6	0	5	4	0.8

WILLIE MCCARTER—DRAKE

| 1971-72 | 39 | 612 | 103 | 257 | .401 | 37 | 55 | .673 | 43 | 85 | 58 | 243 | 6.2 |

STAN MCKENZIE—NEW YORK UNIVERSITY

1970-71	82	2290	398	902	.441	331	396	.836	309	235	238	1127	13.7
1971-72	82	2036	410	834	.492	315	379	.831	272	148	240	1135	13.8
1972-73	7	107	13	36	.361	14	16	.875	21	8	15	40	5.7

JIM MCMILLAN—COLUMBIA

| 1978-79 | 23 | 278 | 33 | 74 | .446 | 17 | 21 | .810 | 39 | 33 | 18 | 83 | 3.6 |

DORIE MURREY—DETROIT

| 1970-71 | 2 | 20 | 1 | 6 | .167 | 9 | 11 | .818 | 7 | 1 | 3 | 11 | 5.5 |

LLOYD NEAL—TENNESSEE STATE

1972-73	80	2723	455	921	.494	187	293	.638	967	146	305	1097	13.4
1973-74	80	1517	246	502	.490	117	168	.696	494	89	190	609	7.6
1974-75	82	2278	409	869	.471	189	295	.641	687	139	239	1007	12.3
1975-76	68	2320	435	904	.481	186	268	.694	585	118	254	1056	15.5
1976-77	58	955	160	340	.471	77	114	.675	255	58	148	397	6.8
1977-78	61	1174	272	540	.504	127	177	.718	373	81	128	671	11.0
1978-79	4	48	4	11	.364	1	1	1.000	9	1	7	9	2.3

WILLIE NORWOOD—ALCORN A & M

| 1977-78 | 19 | 351 | 40 | 99 | .404 | 30 | 46 | .652 | 65 | 19 | 56 | 110 | 5.8 |

TOM OWENS—SOUTH CAROLINA

1977–78	82	1714	313	639	.490	206	278	.741	541	160	263	832	10.1
1978–79	82	2791	600	1095	.548	320	403	.794	740	301	329	1520	18.5

GEOFF PETRIE—PRINCETON

1970–71	82	3032	784	1770	.443	463	600	.722	280	390	196	2031	24.8
1971–72	60	2155	465	1115	.417	202	256	.789	133	248	108	1132	18.9
1972–73	79	3134	836	1801	.464	298	383	.778	273	350	163	1970	24.9
1973–74	73	2800	740	1537	.481	291	341	.853	208	315	199	1771	24.3
1974–75	80	3109	602	1319	.456	261	311	.839	209	424	215	1465	18.3
1975–76	72	2557	543	1177	.461	277	334	.829	168	330	194	1363	18.9

RICK ROBERSON—CINCINNATI

1973–74	69	2060	364	797	.457	205	316	.649	701	133	252	933	13.5

DALE SCHLUETER—COLORADO STATE

1970–71	80	1823	257	527	.488	143	218	.656	629	192	265	657	8.2
1971–72	81	2693	353	672	.525	241	326	.739	860	285	277	927	11.7
1977–78	10	109	8	19	.421	9	18	.500	21	18	20	25	2.5

MARK SIBLEY—NORTHWESTERN

1973–74	28	124	20	56	.357	6	7	.857	25	13	23	46	1.6

BILL SMITH—SYRACUSE

1971–72	22	448	72	173	.416	38	64	.594	135	19	73	182	8.3

Season												
1972-73	76	1610	234	485	.482	75	128	.586	383	122	218	543	7.1
1973-74	67	878	99	228	.434	48	79	.608	189	78	126	246	3.7
1974-75	55	519	72	147	.490	32	48	.667	89	27	96	174	3.2
1975-76	1	3	0	1	.000	0	0	.000	0	0	2	0	0.0

WILLIE SMITH—MISSOURI

Season												
1978-79	13	131	23	44	.523	12	17	.706	13	17	19	58	4.5

LARRY STEELE—KENTUCKY

Season												
1971-72	72	1311	148	308	.481	70	97	.722	282	161	198	366	5.1
1972-73	66	1301	159	329	.483	71	89	.798	154	156	181	389	5.9
1973-74	81	2648	325	680	.478	135	171	.789	310	323	295	785	9.7
1974-75	76	2389	265	484	.548	122	146	.836	227	287	254	652	8.6
1975-76	81	2382	322	651	.495	154	203	.759	292	324	289	798	9.9
1976-77	81	1680	326	652	.500	183	227	.806	188	172	216	835	10.3
1977-78	65	1132	210	447	.470	100	122	.820	113	87	138	520	8.0
1978-79	72	1488	203	483	.420	112	136	.834	171	142	208	518	7.2

BILL STRICKER—PACIFIC

Season												
1970-71	1	2	2	3	.667	0	0	.000	0	0	1	4	4.0

IRA TERRELL—SOUTHERN METHODIST

Season												
1978-79	18	160	30	54	.556	8	15	.533	37	15	27	68	3.8

MYCHAL THOMPSON—MINNESOTA

Season												
1978-79	73	2144	460	938	.490	154	269	.572	604	176	270	1074	14.7

BILL TURNER—AKRON

Season												
1972-73	2	8	2	6	.333	0	0	.000	2	0	3	4	2.0

DAVE TWARDZIK—OLD DOMINION

1976–77	74	1937	263	430	.612	239	284	.842	202	247	228	765	10.3
1977–78	75	1820	242	409	.592	183	234	.782	133	244	186	667	8.9
1978–79	64	1570	203	381	.533	261	299	.873	119	176	185	667	10.4

BOB VERGA—DUKE

1973–74	21	216	42	93	.452	20	32	.625	18	17	22	104	5.0

WALLY WALKER—VIRGINIA

1976–77	67	627	137	305	.449	67	100	.670	108	51	92	341	5.1
1977–78	9	101	19	41	.463	5	8	.625	18	8	13	43	4.8

BILL WALTON—UCLA

1974–75	35	1153	177	345	.513	94	137	.686	441	167	115	448	12.8
1975–76	51	1687	345	732	.471	133	228	.583	681	220	144	821	16.1
1976–77	65	2264	491	930	.528	228	327	.697	934	245	174	1210	18.6
1977–78	58	1929	460	882	.522	177	246	.720	766	291	145	1097	18.9

SIDNEY WICKS—UCLA

1971–72	82	3245	784	1837	.427	441	621	.710	943	350	186	2009	24.5
1972–73	80	3152	761	1684	.452	384	531	.723	870	440	253	1906	23.8
1973–74	75	2853	685	1492	.459	314	412	.762	684	326	214	1684	22.5
1974–75	82	3162	692	1391	.497	394	558	.706	877	287	289	1778	21.9
1975–76	79	3044	580	1201	.483	345	512	.674	712	244	250	1505	19.1

				LENNY WILKINS—PROVIDENCE					
1974–75	65	1161	134	305	.439	152	198	.768	120	235	96	420	6.5

				DAVE WOHL—PENNSYLVANIA					
1972–73	22	393	47	114	.412	24	33	.727	20	68	45	118	5.4

				CHARLES YELVERTON—FORDHAM					
1971–72	69	1227	206	530	.389	133	188	.707	201	81	145	545	7.9